THIS WE BELIEVE

THIS WE BELIEVE

Eight Truths Presbyterians Affirm

Stephen W. Plunkett

Geneva Press
Louisville, Kentucky

Scripture quotations from the New Revised Standard Version of the Bible are copyright © 1989 by the Division of Christian Education of the National Council of the Churches of Christ in the U.S.A. and are used by permission.

Scripture quotations from the Revised Standard Version of the Bible are copyright © 1946, 1952, 1971, and 1973 by the Division of Christian Education of the National Council of the Churches of Christ in the U.S.A. and are used by permission.

Hymn 217 from *The Presbyterian Hymnal,* © 1927 The Presbyterian Committee of Publication. Used by permission of Westminster John Knox Press.

Hymns 31, 41, 92, 101, 102, 171, 260, 280, 394, 438, 442, 457, 478, and 546 from *The Presbyterian Hymnal: Hymns, Psalms, and Spiritual Songs,* © 1990 Westminster John Knox Press. Used by permission of Westminster John Knox Press.

Hymns 191, 289, and 383 from *The Hymnbook,* © 1955 by John Ribble; renewed 1983. Used by permission of Westminster John Knox Press.

Excerpts from *Christian Doctrine* by Shirley Guthrie, © 1994 Shirley C. Guthrie. Used by permission of Westminster John Knox Press.

Excerpts from *The Cocktail Party,* © 1950 by T. S. Eliot and renewed 1978 by Esme Valerie Eliot. Reprinted by permission of Harcourt, Inc.

"The Creation," from *God's Trombones* by James Weldon Johnson, © 1927 The Viking Press, Inc., renewed © 1955 by Grace Nail Johnson. Used by permission of Viking Penguin, a division of Penguin Putnam Inc.

Excerpt from "For the Time Being," from *Collected Poems* by W. H. Auden, reprinted by permission of Faber and Faber Ltd.

Excerpts from *Church Dogmatics* by Karl Barth are reproduced by permission of T & T Clark Publishers, Edinburgh.

Book design by Sharon Adams
Cover design by Lisa Buckley
Cover illustration courtesy of EyeWire

First edition
Published by Geneva Press
Louisville, Kentucky

This book is printed on acid-free paper that meets the American National Standards Institute Z39.48 standard. ⊗

PRINTED IN THE UNITED STATES OF AMERICA

04 05 06 07 08 09 10 11 — 10 9 8 7 6 5 4

Library of Congress Cataloging-in-Publication Data

Plunkett, Stephen W.
    This we believe : eight truths Presbyterians affirm / Stephen W. Plunkett.— 1st ed.
      p. cm.
    Includes bibliographical references.
    ISBN 0-664-50211-3 (pbk.: alk. paper)
      1. Presbyterian Church—Doctrines. I. Title.
BX9175.3 .P57 2002
230'.051—dc21

2001051223

This book is gratefully dedicated to
Margaret,
a devoted wife and mother,
my best friend,
a fellow disciple in the service of Jesus Christ,
a gift of grace.

Acknowledgments

A project of this kind owes its life to many people without whose help it would never have been finished. I extend my deepest thanks to the session and members of St. Andrew Presbyterian Church, Denton, Texas, for their enthusiastic and generous support. In early 2001, they graciously gave me an extended study leave that enabled me to complete a major portion of the book. I also thank Robert M. Shelton for welcoming me to the Austin Presbyterian Theological Seminary community during that study leave, as well as the library staff for making me feel at home. And I am grateful to Thomas W. Gillespie and the library staff at Princeton Theological Seminary for extending the courtesies of the seminary to me during January of 2000.

I can never repay the debt of those who gave their time to read my manuscript and offer their critiques which, in every case, were enlightening and helpful. They are Fred W. Cassell, Thomas W. Currie Jr., Thomas W. Currie III, George S. Heyer Jr., George W. Stroup, and two colleagues with whom I have the privilege of working each day, Clint Loveall and Lisa Patterson. Their helpful comments greatly improved the finished product, and I am thankful for the theological discussion and reflection that their critiques provided. I also thank Elizabeth Achtemeier for her reading of "Laying the Foundation: Getting the Bible Whole" and for her helpful critique that strengthened that chapter. And my gratitude goes to Sue Russell, another colleague at St. Andrew Presbyterian Church, for helping me so generously with the mounds of paperwork that were generated in preparing the manuscript.

Most of all, however, I thank my family for putting up with me throughout what must have seemed like an interminable project. That alone testifies to the perseverance of the saints! My gratitude goes to Margaret, Stephen, and Alison for reading and critiquing the manuscript and, additionally, to Margaret for proofreading, for getting the permissions needed for quotations, and for constantly being available with her solidly Reformed theological instinct and perspective. Especially, however, I thank all three for their encouragement at every step along the way. They daily show me the grace of God in our midst, and I thank them from the bottom of my heart.

Contents

Introduction
Forgotten Truth

A View from the Trenches

These reflections are rooted in a sturdy and tenacious hope for the renewal of the church. Unfortunately, however, turmoil and uncertainty have hurled us into the twenty-first century, and our resulting environment feels anything but hopeful. Many people today experience the church as a brutal battleground of advocacy groups waging ideological warfare and endlessly politicking for the soul of the church. The reflections in this book endeavor to move the discussion away from the tangled web of denominational plots and politics toward the life of the congregation, where ordinary pastors and parishioners wrestle together with what it means to be faithful to Jesus Christ in a complex world of fiercely competing claims.

This book is written for the person in the pew who wrestles week in and week out with the terrors of life in light of the gospel of Jesus Christ and who looks to the church for sustenance and strength only to find it plagued by a fog of confusion. We no longer seem to know what we believe and why we believe it, what the church's fundamental mission is, and how the faith of the Bible relates to such everyday issues as holding our marriages together, raising our children, and being persons of integrity in the workplace. This book endeavors to help us return to the basics of the Christian faith and to regain a degree of clarity about what it means to belong to our faithful Savior Jesus Christ both in life and in death. My hope is that it will furnish an occasion to revisit the story of the Bible or, in some instances, to visit it for the first time.

The view from the trenches is not a pretty scene. Membership rolls have plummeted for nearly four decades; worn-out organizational structures no longer work; trust in regional and national church leaders has eroded to an all-time low; and pastors and congregations are increasingly deadlocked in the stalemate of conflict. The language of the historic Christian faith is often arrogantly brushed aside in favor of a more "user-friendly" vocabulary that studiously avoids any suggestion of sacrifice or self-denial—anything that runs the risk of appearing demanding or judgmental. More and more, our life is centered not in the proclamation of Jesus Christ, crucified and risen, but in the maintenance of an institution.

This book is written from the conviction that the church today faces a theological crisis of faith and obedience. Some would have us believe that our window into the future is better planning and fund-raising, or perhaps more effective strategies for church growth. Yet such flimsy Band-Aids only illustrate how dense and blinding the fog can be—as if the woes of the church could be solved by another committee meeting or strategy (or even another book on the truths Presbyterians affirm!).

The special-interest advocacy groups that besiege today's church also offer no shortage of solutions to our problems, only to end up being a major part of the problem themselves. For example, does the agenda of ideological feminism hold the answer? Shall we be saved from the pitfalls ensnaring the church, not to mention the whole of human society, if we just call a spade a spade and admit that patriarchy is the root of all evil and then work like the devil to stamp it out? Would this produce the church of God's future? Or maybe the answer is properly balanced God-language. Should God be called Father or Mother? She or he? Yes, maybe the church will experience renewal if we just wake up and get the pronouns right! Or is the key to the future God has in mind a more intentionally legislated balance of gender and race on our committees and governing bodies? Indeed, many would have us believe that such a carefully engineered inclusiveness is precisely God's answer to the riddle of the ages. Others, however, plead for the church to return to "the good old days" when life was simple and faith uncomplicated. But are we really to believe that the key to God's future is recapturing the essence of some golden age vaguely remembered?

All of these special-interest agendas contain elements of the truth that we need both to hear and to heed. For example, patriarchy resulted in the centuries-old exclusion of women from positions of leadership and the denigration of the God-given gifts of women. If feminism means equality between women and men in every sphere of life, including the ministry of the church, then every Christian by nature is a feminist. After all, in Jesus Christ there is no longer Jew or Greek, slave or free, male or female, for all are one in Christ Jesus (Gal. 3:28). Furthermore, I have seen firsthand in my adult church school class that the exclusive use of male language for God has communicated, however unwittingly, the unbiblical view that God is male. Several years ago, I prepared an essay on God-language and presented it to my class. I was astonished that several members were absolutely stunned to learn that their pastor does not believe

God is male! Furthermore, the church is a long, long way from the cosmic, universal community of all races and nations foretold in the gospel: "[A]nd there was a great multitude from every nation, from all tribes and peoples and languages, standing before the throne and before the Lamb" (Rev. 7:9).

A major problem, however, arises when any individual or group insists that the entire life of the church be forced through its narrowly defined ideological filter; and, in today's church, this insistence comes not only with brutal regularity but with unrestrained vehemence. Anyone who possesses even a cursory knowledge of church history and is remotely realistic about the nature of human sin knows that all such answers are doomed to failure. There is no program, plan, or schema that will renew the church. Genuine renewal is entirely the gift of God's grace given exclusively in Jesus Christ. In the words of Karl Barth, "We are . . . not yet obedient, or no longer so, if the court to which we are finally responsible is a system, a program, a statute, a method, an 'ism,' no matter whether it be philosophical, political, or theological, static or dynamic, conservative, liberal, or authoritarian, or even Christian. Even at best an 'ism' . . . is not God's Word nor can it replace this."[1]

What, then, would be an appropriate response for such a time as this? The answer comes as we face up to the underlying causes of our spiritual malaise. Much of what bedevils the church today is rooted in the twin maladies of biblical illiteracy and theological amnesia. In 1970, James D. Smart wrote a book entitled *The Strange Silence of the Bible in the Church*.[2] His title accurately summarizes how the church has veered so radically off course, with the Bible growing more and more silent in the ensuing years. The strange thing, of course, is that the Bible is silent of all places in the church, the very community that God has gathered around the Word. If the truth be told, most of us no longer know even the basic content of the story of the Bible—its main characters and events and the general flow of biblical history. Similarly, for the average church member, the content of the sixteenth-century Reformation[3] has about as much authority as the yellow pages of the local phone book. "So what?" some people ask. "What do those obscure names and places have to do with my life in the real world today?"

The Heidelberg Catechism begins with the question "What is your only comfort, in life and in death?" And the answer is simply but powerfully stated: "That I belong—body and soul, in life and in death—not to myself but to my faithful Savior, Jesus Christ."[4] From much the same perspective, our ancestor in the faith, John Calvin, once wrote,

> We are not our own: let not our reason nor our will, therefore, sway our plans and deeds. We are not our own: let us therefore not set it as our goal

to seek what is expedient for us according to the flesh. We are not our own: in so far as we can, let us therefore forget ourselves and all that is ours. Conversely, we are God's: let us therefore live for him and die for him. We are God's: let his wisdom and will therefore rule all our actions.[5]

The culture of self-realization, which is as commonplace to Americans as the air we breathe, has taught us that the most important questions in life are questions such as "Who am I? What do I want to get out of life? And what is it that will give me an endless measure of personal happiness?" Much to the contrary, disciples of Jesus Christ, whose lives are built on the foundation of the Bible and the tradition of the Reformation, know that there are far more important questions to ask, such as "*Whose* am I? How am I called to live as a person who belongs not to myself but to Jesus Christ? And how can I serve God in my small corner of the world, even when serving God requires personal sacrifice and self-denial?"

The way we think, speak, and live form a living record of how we have framed the major questions of life. Is my life my own property? The world believes it is. American culture believes it is. The daily news is saturated with stories of people who have said, "Yes, my life is unquestionably my own property, and I'll live it as I please, thank you very much. I have a right to happiness as *I* define happiness, and I'll take it however I can get it—no matter whose heart gets broken or whose dignity gets trampled on. To hell with any higher authority than myself!" But disciples of Jesus Christ, whose lives are grounded in the lavishly gracious story of the Bible, are called to tell and to live a different story. We know that we belong not to ourselves but to the risen Christ, who is both our Savior and *the living Lord of our lives*. A life lived from this vantage point is radically different because personal decisions rooted in the lordship of Jesus Christ are decidedly at odds with the pursuit of happiness in American culture where we find ourselves, more often than not, swimming against the stream. *Yet we are unable even to glimpse this radically divergent vantage point apart from the story of salvation God has given us in the Bible.*

A personal illustration helps to make the point. I remember sitting down one evening several years ago with a group of young people who were preparing for Youth Sunday. Peter's confession that Jesus is the Christ, found in Mark 8, was our focus, so in an effort to help them understand this affirmation of faith, I probed a bit to see what they grasped of the Old Testament expectation that God would send a messiah. When it became clear that the word "messiah" meant nothing to them, I began to broaden my probe to include the biblical story in general. "Can you name some of the kings of Israel that we read about in the Old Testament?" I asked. They couldn't. Finally, King David did ring a bell for some, but only after I first mentioned his name. "What do you remember about the promised land?" I continued. Nothing. The concept meant absolutely nothing to them. I was stunned. These were children of the covenant who had made it all the way to high school, and they (1) knew nothing of the Old Testament expectation of a messiah, (2) were unable to name on their own any of the kings of Israel, and (3) had not the foggiest idea what the concept of the promised land was all about. And none of this falls in the category of obscure information! Every one of these young people had been baptized and confirmed, but I found myself asking, "Baptized into what? Confirmed as what?"

I am not suggesting that every member of the church, by the time she or he is in the tenth grade, should be able to write a master's thesis on the Bible. But I am suggesting that the message of the Bible is absolutely central to the faith and mission of the church, and the current lack of familiarity with it is devastating. It is devastating to worship, to Christian education, to the church's sense of mission, to the understanding our elders and deacons bring to their work as church officers, and to every sphere of the church's life. And it becomes particularly devastating in the context of warring ideological factions. When the story of the Bible is missing, all kinds of "plausible arguments" and "empty deceit, according to human tradition" (Col. 2:4, 8) will fill the void.

"Our people, as a rule, do not read the Bible, in any sense which makes its language more familiar and dear to them than the language of the novel or the press,"[6] wrote P. T. Forsyth in the early years of the twentieth century, and this problem only multiplied in the ensuing years. Elizabeth Achtemeier reflects on the church in our day at the dawn of a new millennium:

> Through 30 years of teaching in seminaries I have become convinced that the church has largely failed in its mission of educating its people in the apostolic, biblical faith. Every preacher who enters a pulpit these days must assume that the congregation knows almost nothing about the content of the Scriptures. The language of faith, the meaning of the sacraments and the basic doctrines of the Christian church are almost totally devoid of meaning for the average church-goer. Thus our congregations are often at the mercy of the latest kooky cult, . . . and there is no common biblical story that binds them together in their faith. Individuals drift from one church to another, without roots, without religious history, without any Rock or Refuge or any sense that they belong to a communion of saints or participate in an ongoing history of salvation that God is working out in their lives and world.[7]

Perhaps this is why it has come to the point where even the secular press observes, "Not only are the traditional denominations failing to get their message across; they are increasingly unsure just what that message is."[8]

With this in mind, consider the case of a woman who made an appointment to see me one day. After discussing a couple of other matters, she broached the real issue that led her to my study. She explained that she had been a Christian all of her adult life but still didn't know the basic story of the Bible. "How can I correct this?" she wanted to know. I was immensely thankful that she gave me the privilege of helping, but I was also saddened that, many years after her baptism, she still hadn't pieced together the basic story of salvation that forms the heart of the Christian faith. There are, of course, numerous possible reasons for this, not the least of which is the fact that several generations of teaching elders (i.e., ministers of the Word and Sacrament) have abandoned their role as teachers in the congregation. But let's not miss another of the more glaring reasons. The church today thinks it can be the church apart from the story of the Bible. We mainline Christians have done everything at church except tell the story. We have gone through the motions of liturgy and creed and have hotly debated every social issue under the sun, but the basic needs of the human soul have not been met. Apparently, it is possible for a person to go through all the motions of congregational life without hearing and internalizing the one story that conveys to the world the message of salvation in Jesus Christ. It is no wonder the mainline churches in America are in decline and in need of reformation.

It is as though we are foolishly trying to build a house without a foundation, which is precisely the point Herbert O'Driscoll makes by suggesting that "much contemporary preaching is like a highrise developer deciding to commence building at the fifth floor on the assumption that the first four floors and the basement are already in place."[9] The first four floors and the basement are decidedly *not* in place, and the most pressing job we face is starting over and rebuilding from the basement up. O'Driscoll continues by saying that the first four floors and the basement "of Christian faith have been devastated by the cultural earthquakes and events of this century. The vocation of preachers today is to lay the basement floor again, to lay the foundations of faith again."[10]

This pressing need has surfaced in my own ministry through a variety of personal encounters that continue to haunt me. Picture, if you will, an adult Bible study in progress. The leader asks the participants to turn to Philippians, whereupon a longtime ordained elder looks rather tentatively at the ominous volume in his hand before thumbing aimlessly through the Old Testament for Paul's letter.

Or picture a young confirmand at the historic Presbyterian church of a certain city smack in the middle of the Bible belt. When asked if she knows herself to be a sinner in the sight of God, justly deserving God's wrath and without hope except in God's sovereign mercy, she replies in rather startled fashion, "No, I've never thought of myself that way!" This lovely young girl from one of the community's finest families had managed to make it all the way to adolescence without learning one of the most basic realities of the Christian faith, namely, that without God's love in Jesus Christ forgiving our sins and calling us to new life, none of us has so much as a single shred of hope.

Or ponder with me a situation I faced one year with a young confirmand who didn't even know the method of execution that was used to kill Jesus. His pastors, parents, and church family had somehow never helped him make the connection between the cross in the chancel and his salvation in Jesus Christ. What exactly was the content of the faith in which he was preparing to be confirmed?

In a secular world where practically everything is in flux and precious little remains the same, where the very foundations of our civilization often appear to be crumbling, we need to know not just who we are, but *whose* we are. We learn whose we are in the mass of wounded humanity, gathered like lost sheep at the foot of the cross and given undeserved yet lavish forgiveness. The Bible teaches us this good news as nothing else does, as nothing else can. It is not a mere luxury for those who have the time and inclination to learn it. Neither is it simply an intellectual hobby for those who find ancient texts a curiosity worth exploring. The Bible is essential for the faith of the cross and for willing surrender to the Christ who says, "If any want to become my followers, let them deny themselves and take up their cross and follow me" (Mark 8:34).

Tradition vs. Traditionalism

I remember a conversation I once had with a group of Presbyterian pastors in which I argued, as I have just done, that a return to the Bible and the Reformed tradition is essential for the renewal of the church. It surprises me still that, for some in the group, my argument automatically translated into a dead faith all wrapped up in learning the right vocabulary and mastering a body of data. It was seen as rigid and inflexible, a precise illustration of what the church does not need.

Why is it that people's hackles are raised the moment someone mentions the word *tradition*? For many people, tradition is indeed like unto a four-letter word, smacking of a head trip and suggesting an inordinate reverence for the past. There is, of course, an approach to the Bible and tradition that is stifling and dead, and, unfortunately, many of us have experienced some version of that approach. But this is not about an intellectual head trip that worships the past and epitomizes everything that is religiously intractable, and it is not about worshiping the Bible and tradition. It is about worshiping and serving the God who is uniquely revealed in the Bible and communicated to us in a vital and living way through our tradition as Reformed Christians. As John Leith reminds us, "Tradition is the living faith of dead people. Traditionalism is the dead faith of living people. For this reason tradition is a source of the church's vitality and traditionalism the occasion of its death."[11]

Each year when new elders and deacons are elected in my congregation, I tell them that, for us Presbyterians, the Reformed tradition is our way of being Christian, and since they have been elected to lead the congregation in the service of Jesus Christ, they need to have a grasp of the theological core of our tradition. One year, toward the end of officer training, an elder who had served on the session three or four times previously told me that this was the first time in her experience that officer training had taught her anything about the theological beliefs of the Reformed tradition. She recalled that, in the past, officer training had been a sort of "welcome-to-the-session" approach with a bit of polity thrown in for good measure. Another year, an elder who had served on the session in two previous congregations admitted that, until then, he had not been aware that the *Book of Confessions* even existed. Do not be deceived. The situation today is not one where people are hemmed in by an intractable tradition. Tradition has been all but thrown out, forgotten. How can a tradition that is little known in the congregation be seen as a stifling and oppressive burden?

This is not a call to traditionalism whereby we retreat into the deep recesses of the past. The hope expressed here is born of the promise that the story of the Bible and the tradition of the Reformation are God-given and Christ-centered, the gracious gift of the Holy Spirit for the living of these days. They are indispensable sources of divine revelation for the vision and courage we need to see God more clearly and to follow the living Christ more closely today and in every tomorrow.

We do not, after all, learn the Bible and theology just to carry in our brains an impressive data bank of facts, information, and biblical trivia. Rather, in the story of the Bible and in theology, *we encounter Jesus Christ*, and from him we learn to internalize the substance of Christian discipleship so that it becomes part of the essential fabric of our lives, a living declaration of the crucified and risen Lord of life. In the Reformed tradition, the study of theology has always had a distinctively practical bent. John Calvin, for example, wrote theology not in the ivory tower of the academy but while facing the daily demands of preaching, teaching, and ministering to the pastoral needs of a congregation. *We learn the Bible and theology because the way of obedience to Jesus Christ is opened up in and through them and because they lavish upon us the treasures of God's living grace.* We learn them because they bring us face to face with the Good Shepherd, who never stops reaching out to the lost, and because the recurring theme in all of our lives is

> Perverse and foolish oft I strayed,
> But yet in love He sought me,
> And on His shoulder gently laid,
> And home, rejoicing, brought me.[12]

And we learn them because they lead us to the foot of the cross where Jesus Christ encounters us with both the cost and the joy of discipleship.

Hope at the Crossroads:
Jesus Christ the Center

What follows is one pastor's attempt in his time and place to respond to the crisis at hand by offering a word of hope for the future. The good news of the gospel is that we do not have to be prisoners of our past mistakes and failures and, on the foundation of God's amazing forgiveness, we are set free to build a new future. These reflections do indeed come from the trenches of church life where ordinary Christians grapple with the triumphs and tragedies of the human journey. They come from the mind and heart of a pastor whose life is devoted to preparing and preaching sermons, celebrating the sacraments, teaching classes on Bible and theology, visiting the sick, burying the dead, ministering to the bereaved, counseling couples about to be married, attending endless committee meetings, administering the programs of the church, and, in and through it all, attempting to respond with Christian judgment and grace to the joys and sorrows, the foibles and successes of a congregation. As a lifelong Presbyterian who has been a pastor for more than twenty years, I write with unabashed gratitude for my roots in the Reformed tradition and with vigorous hope that the Word of God will continually reform the church.

In addition to a chapter on the one story of the Bible, I have chosen eight beliefs or doctrines that form a kind of ABCs of the Christian faith. These eight doctrines are in no way intended as a systematic theology or an exhaustive exploration of the essential tenets of the Christian faith. Rather, my much more modest intention is simply to engage folks in thought, conversation, and prayer concerning the message of the Bible, our theological heritage as Reformed Christians, and the culture in which we live.

At the heart of these reflections is the vigorous conviction that Jesus Christ is our only hope. In truth, what the church needs today is nothing less than a miracle of his redeeming love. For this reason, I have attempted to emphasize the centrality of Jesus Christ, not in a single chapter, but throughout the book. The driving conviction behind each of the following eight truths is the joyous word that Jesus Christ is "the way, and the truth, and the life" through whom "God was pleased to reconcile to himself all things, whether on earth or in heaven, by making peace through the blood of his cross" (John 14:6; Col. 1:20). He is the living Christ, who stands before the church and the world with outstretched arms of mercy, ever ready to forgive and renew us with the love that will never let us go. His is the voice that says,

> Come to me, all you that are weary and are carrying heavy burdens, and I will give you rest. Take my yoke upon you, and learn from me; for I am gentle and humble in heart, and you will find rest for your souls. For my yoke is easy, and my burden is light. (Matt. 11:28–30)

Laying the Foundation

Getting the Bible Whole

> *One generation shall laud your works to another, and shall
> declare your mighty acts.*
>
> (Ps. 145:4)

One of the hymns I grew up singing was a quaint old hymn called "I
Love to Tell the Story." Sentimental and soupy by today's standards, it
is not at all the kind of politically correct hymn that is in vogue. But its
words still live in my memory:

> I love to tell the story of unseen things above,
> Of Jesus and His glory, of Jesus and His love.
> I love to tell the story, because I know 'tis true;
> It satisfies my longings as nothing else could do.[1]

We Christians are called to laud God's works from generation to generation by telling the story of the God who has redeemed us in Jesus
Christ. We tell the story because we know it is true as nothing else is true,
and because it untangles us from the intricate web of lies at the heart of
our self-absorbed culture. In the sixth chapter of Deuteronomy, we read,

> Hear, O Israel: The LORD is our God, the LORD alone. You shall love
> the LORD your God with all your heart, and with all your soul, and
> with all your might. Keep these words that I am commanding you
> today in your heart. Recite them to your children and talk about them
> when you are at home and when you are away, when you lie down and
> when you rise. Bind them as a sign on your hand, fix them as an
> emblem on your forehead, and write them on the doorposts of your
> house and on your gates. (Deut. 6:4–9)

This is our divine calling, yet where is the evidence that we have kept
God's Word in our hearts? Is it part of our daily conversation among
family and friends? Is there any living proof that obedience to the Word
of God is the chief ambition and driving force of our lives?

11

Over the past several years, I have become convinced that one of the most formidable challenges facing congregations today, and indeed one of the causes of biblical illiteracy, is the fact that most of our members have experienced the Bible as a random anthology of unrelated texts. Many of our members confess to home Bible reading either infrequently or never, so their only exposure to the biblical story is in Sunday school and/or worship where they get it in tiny bits and pieces—an isolated slice of Israel's history one week and a miracle of Jesus the next. But the fact is, while the sixty-six books of the Bible from Genesis through Revelation contain many, many stories, together they proclaim the single story of God's indestructible love for all creation. A snippet here and a quotable quote there simply are not enough to sustain us through the battering storms of life and to bind up the bruised and wounded. The *whole* story of salvation, on the other hand, has power enough to do just that and, in doing so, to transform our lives—changing us from self-indulgent creatures whose main purpose is looking out for "Number One" into faithful servants of the Servant Lord. The purpose of becoming more biblically literate, once again, is not to accumulate a mental potpourri of biblical times and characters but to lay a sturdy foundation on which to build the Christian life. So before we go any further, let us put all the bits and pieces together into the whole story of God's love that "satisfies our longings as nothing else could do." The narrative as I present it here admittedly omits a great deal. Yet here is the basic skeleton of the story—one way to see the whole of scripture as it forms the single melody of God's matchless love for the redemption of the world.

The One Story of the Bible

In the beginning, *God* . . . God is the central character of the Bible—not human beings and the travail of our precarious plight, not human ideals and aspirations, but the one, true, living God beside whom there is no other.

In the beginning, before the dawn of human civilization, God created everything that is. Out of the vast and endless chaos of nothingness, God gave life, order, and beauty to the universe. The story of the Bible begins with the most magnificent symphony imaginable of God's unlimited power and grace, as God effortlessly speaks the universe into existence. A soaring melody resounds throughout every part of this symphonic masterpiece: "And God said . . . and it was so! And God said . . . and it was so!" God said, "Let there be light . . . let the oceans and dry land appear . . . let there be plants yielding seed and fruit trees of every kind . . . let there be fish in the sea and birds in the air . . . let there be living creatures of every kind—cattle and wild animals and creeping things. . . ." *And it was so!*

The creation of the first human being, however, is a moment without parallel. In the most personal, intimate way conceivable, God kneels down in the dirt of creation and personally scoops together the first human being from the dust of the earth. Then God breathes into his nostrils the breath of life, and he becomes a living being. This act of God reveals one of the most significant things human beings know about themselves: *Human life is rooted in the intention and power of the sovereign God.* Most modern people believe they were born simply because a mother's egg was fertilized by a father's sperm through the human act of procreation. But in addition to the biological claim surrounding human birth, there is supremely a theological claim, namely, that this is God's world, and human beings are given life by God's gracious design and purpose. Without God's breath breathed into us, there would be no life! The psalmist would one day say it this way: "Know that the LORD is God. It is he that made us, and we are his" (Ps. 100:3). The African-American poet James Weldon Johnson offers this powerful depiction based on the story of creation in Genesis 2:

> Up from the bed of the river
> God scooped the clay;
> And by the bank of the river
> He kneeled him down;
> And there the great God Almighty
> Who lit the sun and fixed it in the sky,
> Who flung the stars to the most far corner of the night,
> Who rounded the earth in the middle of his hand;
> This Great God,
> Like a mammy bending over her baby,
> Kneeled down in the dust
> Toiling over a lump of clay
> Till he shaped it in his own image;
> Then into it he blew the breath of life,
> And man became a living soul.
> Amen. Amen.[2]

"Like a mammy bending over her baby . . ." That is the gracious, loving portrayal of God with which the human journey begins.

In all creation, however, a suitable partner for the man is not found. So the Lord God causes a deep sleep to fall upon him and, as he sleeps, God takes one of the man's ribs and creates from it a woman. It is a moment of exquisite ecstasy, for God has now created the perfect partner for the man! "Therefore a man leaves his father and his mother and clings to his wife, and they become one flesh" (Gen. 2:24). And we know that man and woman are created for community with each other.

Unlike all of God's other creatures, man and woman are set apart in yet another exceptional way: *We have been created in the image of God.* That is, human beings have been given a dignity as well as the ability of moral decision[3] not possessed by other creatures. Man and woman mirror God to the world and act as representatives of God[4] in a way that other creatures do not. Inherent in this God-given role is a responsibility unique in all of God's creation to the human being. God calls the human race to live as divinely appointed servants and stewards, and to exercise power on earth just as God exercises power, not with tyranny and exploitation but as trusted stewards who are friends of creation.[5]

Such was the magnificent creation that God pronounced "very good." God's relationship with man and woman and their environment was a source of abundant delight for God. And what's more, man and woman were created to delight both in God and in each other.

God was soon to be robbed of this joy, however. The first man and woman wanted for nothing, because God's will for them was sheer grace, untarnished love, abundant life. God placed Adam and Eve in a garden called Eden and promised to provide in superabundance for their every need. Not only was Eden beautiful to behold, but it provided everything they would need to sustain and enjoy life. The trees of the garden with their plentiful fruit were there for Adam's and Eve's daily sustenance and well-being. There was, however, one prohibition. Adam and Eve were commanded by God not to eat of the tree of the knowledge of good and evil because, in the day that they ate of it, God assured them, they would surely die. Adam and Eve had prodigious freedom, but not unlimited freedom, not freedom as a blank check. Part of living in faithful relation to their Creator was accepting their creaturehood by living on God's terms and accepting their God-given boundaries.

But Adam and Eve soon decided that they preferred their lives to be self-directed rather than God-directed. In fact, they had an unquenchable penchant for the carte blanche variety of freedom, and when push came to shove, they chose autonomy over dependence on God. One day the serpent came into the midst of Eden and asked Eve, "Did God say, 'You shall not eat from any tree in the garden?'" This subtle deception brought the jagged teeth of self-destruction to the very threshold of paradise. The serpent knew full well that God had not imposed such a prohibition. God said they could freely eat of all the trees except one. But now the serpent had introduced fraud into the scene, and the utter betrayal of God was just around the corner.

"No," answered Eve, "God did not forbid us from eating of all the fruit in the garden; God only commanded that we not eat of the tree of the knowledge of good and evil."

"Don't you know why?" teased the serpent. "God doesn't want you to eat of the choicest of all trees because it will make you like God, knowing good and evil." *To be like God! What a deliciously marvelous prospect!* So Adam and Eve, seduced by the enticement of autonomy and aflame with lust for the forbidden fruit, ate of the tree of the knowledge of good and evil. Being a mere creature could be abandoned easily enough; yes, they would seize their self-determined future and be like God. And suddenly their eyes were opened; they knew for the first time that they were naked; and they ran to the bushes, hiding and ashamed.

The entire human story is now ripped apart with disobedience, and the long, ignominious journey toward death commences. Adam and Eve are forever cast out of Eden. They no longer have a safe haven of utter joy and delight in their God and each other. Their rebellion has brought them a life of enmity and strife, of suffering and pain from which they will never escape. Paradise has ended. The relationship of unmarred delight between Creator and creature has been erased from the face of the earth. And the truth that we must not miss is this: The story of Adam and Eve is not merely the tale of two long-ago characters on the dusty page of an ancient text. In biblical Hebrew, *Adam* literally means "humankind," and *Eve* means "the mother of all living." This is not the story of two persons as much as it is the story of every person—of *you* and of *me*—told for the sake of unqualified truthfulness about who we are in the presence of the holy and living God.

The day of rebellion, however, is not without God's grace. First of all, Adam and Eve do not die in the day that they eat of the forbidden tree, and we see from this early moment in the human story that God's nature is long-suffering and God's character is gracious. As Adam and Eve are being banished from Eden with the heavy weight of their sin upon them, the Lord God personally makes for them garments of skins and clothes them. They do not escape punishment for their sin and are destined for the rest of their lives to face the consequences of their rebellion. But God does not desert them. They had utterly abandoned their God, but God refuses utterly to abandon them. In fact, God personally gives them the very protection they will need from the thorns and thistles, the perils and vulnerabilities of life beyond Eden. Yes, the story of how the human creature became the enemy of God comes to an end with God's act of compassion.

The saga of disobedience, however, has only just begun. Very early, we learn that when the vertical relationship with God is broken, the horizontal relationship with other human beings is unavoidably broken as well. Cain murders Abel, and hatred and bigotry become an invasive cancer devouring the human soul as we behold the all-encompassing consequences of sin. In fact, the malignancy of rebellion spreads to uncontrollable proportions until it infects the whole of what God, in the beginning, pronounced "very good."

> The LORD saw that the wickedness of humankind was great in the earth, and that every inclination of the thoughts of their hearts was only evil continually. And the LORD was sorry that he had made humankind on the earth, and it grieved him to his heart. (Gen. 6:5–6)

It is a moment of intense anguish in the heart of God. The sovereign Lord who effortlessly spoke the universe into existence now grieves over the ravaging perversions of the human heart. The God who once leaned over Adam "like a mammy bending over her baby" has been rejected. Finally, in complete sorrow, God determines to obliterate the entire creation.

Yet just as God is on the brink of annihilating the earth and all of its inhabitants, God's eye falls on a man named Noah, who becomes God's hope of a new beginning, the seed of a fresh start. Yes, God will be faithful to creation. Instead of total destruction, creation will be purged of sin and disobedience. The slate will be wiped clean, and the human race will become again what God intended from the beginning—a willing, joyous partner in fellowship with God and other human beings. So God instructs Noah to build a great ark and to take his family and a male and female of every kind of animal inside the ark. Then God causes a great flood to cover the earth and destroy everyone and everything except those safely secured inside the ark. God's purpose was to purify the earth and restore the relationship of trust and obedience for which God yearned and for which human beings were created.

The centuries, however, tell the sad tale that the hope Noah represented was doomed to disaster. The earth was momentarily cleansed, but the heart of the human creature had not changed, and the human race was caught in the relentless grip of sin, leading inescapably to self-destruction and death. When we come to Genesis 11, human pride has swollen out of control. "Come," the human creatures exclaim to each other as the arrogance of human prowess blossoms, "let us build ourselves a city, and a tower with its top in the heavens, and let us make a name for ourselves; otherwise we shall be scattered abroad upon the face of the whole earth" (11:4). They imagine a world in which human power is unlimited, so they begin to build a tower that will enable them to scale the heavens and enter the very realm of God. Like Adam and Eve, their ambition is to be on a par with God; indeed, to be like God. And they will accomplish this great feat on their own, as autonomous human beings. So God confuses their speech and scatters them abroad over the face of the earth.

By now, it is clear that sin against God is not a mere choice for human beings but is endemic to the human condition. But God will not give up. Even when we are faithless, God is faithful; and in answer to our need, God reaches out to all the earth through the family lineage of one man and woman.

In the second millennium B.C., God called Abraham out of Mesopotamia to be the seed of the nation, Israel. God asked Abraham and his wife, Sarah, in their old age, to pack their bags, pull up stakes, and willingly leave behind their country and kindred. They were to embark on a long, circuitous, risk-filled journey toward a promised land. It was to be a peculiar kind of journey because the precise destination was not yet disclosed. There would be no maps given and no promises made of a journey free of hazard and peril. In fact, this would end up being the most perilous kind of journey imaginable because it involved blind yet total trust in the God who called them. In effect, they were asked to relinquish control of their own destiny and place their destiny in the hands of God. This journey would require a leap of faith of gargantuan proportions. Abraham and Sarah knew not what the morrow would bring, but they were assured that God would embrace them through every hazard, provide for every need, and love them through each dark night of the soul that awaited them in the upcoming journey to the land of promise. In establishing this covenant relationship, God promised to be their God and expected in return Abraham's and Sarah's undivided loyalty and total fidelity.

God's promises to Abraham and Sarah seemed an absurd exercise in hoping for the impossible. They were part of a landless class of people, but God promised them land. Both were advanced in age, and Sarah was long past the age of childbearing, but God promised them progeny as numerous as the stars in the heavens. In fact, God's pledge was to make of Abraham and Sarah a great nation by which all the families of the earth would be blessed. The unwavering purpose of God was to reach out to the ends of the earth and reclaim the entire human family through the one nation Israel. God's love would continue to be universal, encompassing all the earth and including all people. This was the special role that Israel was destined to play in the purposes of God.

Instant gratification, however, was not part of the gift. In fact, it literally would be centuries before the promised land was given, and the journey so circuitous that the daughters and sons of Israel would find themselves, generations later, not in a promised land flowing with milk and honey but enslaved in Egypt.

Despite Sarah's barrenness, God kept the promise, and Sarah conceived and bore Isaac, who was the father of Jacob. In the course of time, the sons of Jacob found themselves in Egypt where the Israelites became slaves of Pharaoh. Yet as bleak and hopeless as the situation seemed, God did not forget the promise to Abraham, and neither did God turn a deaf ear to the people's anguished cry for divine deliverance. After 430 years of bondage to Pharaoh, God called a man named Moses to lead the slaves to freedom.

When the time for the march to freedom finally arrived, none of the Hebrew slaves believed it was possible. If they were indeed to be set free, it would be God's doing, for escape long ago ceased to be a human possibility. God commanded Moses to instruct all the Israelites to sacrifice a Passover lamb and put the blood of the lamb on the lintel and two doorposts of each house. At midnight, God promised to strike down the firstborn of all the Egyptians but to pass over every house that had the blood of the Passover lamb on the lintel and doorposts. Midnight came and God kept the promise, slaying all the firstborn in the land of Egypt. Pharaoh, stunned and bereft, lost no time in setting the slaves free and, in a state of panic, the Egyptians even urged the Israelites to hasten their departure lest all the Egyptians be struck down.

But no sooner had their journey to freedom commenced than Pharaoh changed his mind. Quickly, the chariots of Pharaoh were dispatched with his soldiers in hot pursuit of the runaway slaves. Trapped between the ruthless army of Pharaoh behind them and the Red Sea in front of them, the slaves, it appeared, were doomed. Their choice was simple. They could either surrender to Pharaoh and return to slavery, or they could meet their death in the raging waters of the sea. With God, however, nothing is impossible, and just as God opened the womb of Sarah to create a nation, so also God miraculously opened the way for the Israelites' salvation as the menace of destruction loomed all around them. At the decisive moment, God caused the Red Sea to part, creating an avenue of dry land so the Israelites could cross to freedom. The waters of the sea formed a wall both to their left and to their right, as God victoriously led them to salvation and safety. As soon as the Israelites were safely on the other side of the sea, the waters returned to their flow and swallowed the pursuing Egyptians. The slaves were finally free, their liberty graciously given by the God of their creation. Once again, we see that God is utterly faithful. God has not, does not, and will not desert the covenant community.

Free at last, the journey toward the promised land commences in earnest. The Israelites, however, will be required to continue waiting for the fulfillment of God's promise, and as they wait, they are consigned to a long period of wandering in the wilderness around Mt. Sinai, searching for their long-awaited promised land. These desert years stoutly test Israel's willingness to trust God in all the frightening shadows of life. Day by day, the covenant community must learn the thorny lessons of trust and gratitude in the parched, desolate, thirsty wilderness of life.

The testing of Israel, however, is chock-full of bitter disappointment for God. God asks of Abraham and Sarah's progeny no more and no less than God had required of Abraham and Sarah—to embark on a risk-filled journey toward a promised land of undisclosed location, a journey void of maps and fraught with peril, a journey in which they would willingly surrender their destiny into the hands of God. Just as Sarah and Abraham were called, now their great-great-great-great grandchildren are asked to place their trust in this covenant-making, promise-keeping God. The Lord who had redeemed them from slavery now promises to lead them ever onward to the promised land. But the Israelites want the promised land *now*, not later, and they want the journey to be easy, the terrain to be user-friendly. God is calling them to a cross-country trek on foot, but they fancy themselves instead on a holiday cruise. So they whine and gripe and grouse and squawk their way through the wilderness. And the most mind-boggling part of the story is that God resolutely refuses to give up on this stubborn, recalcitrant specimen of the human race.

During the desert years, Israel arrived at the foot of Mount Sinai where the covenant between God and Israel was sealed. The covenant community was called to a new way of life, a life of undivided loyalty to the Lord God who redeemed them from slavery and promised to give them a land flowing with milk and honey. And to show them how to live in covenant faithfulness, God gave them the Ten Commandments:

1. I am the LORD your God, who brought you out of the land of Egypt, out of the house of slavery; you shall have no other gods before me.
2. You shall not make for yourself an idol, whether in the form of anything that is in heaven above or that is on the earth beneath, or that is in the water under the earth. You shall not bow down to them and worship them.
3. You shall not make wrongful use of the name of the LORD your God.
4. Remember the sabbath day, and keep it holy.
5. Honor your father and your mother.
6. You shall not murder.
7. You shall not commit adultery.
8. You shall not steal.
9. You shall not bear false witness against your neighbor.
10. You shall not covet your neighbor's house; you shall not covet your neighbor's wife [spouse], or anything that belongs to your neighbor.
    (from Exod. 20:1–17 and Deut. 5:6–21)

On their way to the land of promise, the covenant people were to learn the ways of God so that they would be free to live in covenant faithfulness. The

Ten Commandments were God's law of love to govern them in their new life—God's word that would protect them from the worship of false gods, preserve them against the perils of disobedience and despair, empower them to live as God's own possession, nurture in them covenant loyalty to God above all other loyalties, and teach them loving respect for their neighbors. Faithfulness to the Ten Commandments would brand Israel as a holy people, set apart by God for the service of God in the world. The law was not given as an onerous burden but as a living and loving source of God's daily grace. It was God's way of saying, "You are my possession, and because you don't know on your own how to live as my covenant people, I will show you."

Yet even as God unfailingly reached out to embrace the covenant community, the sin of Adam and Eve was multiplied ad infinitum in each new generation. *To be like God! What a deliciously marvelous prospect!* To live as independent, autonomous, self-governing creatures, answerable to no authority other than the self—this became the all-consuming passion of the human heart. God willed only goodness, but the human will was knotted with callous disobedience at every turn. Yet once again the sustaining melody of the story was God's unfaltering faithfulness in the midst of obstinate, intractable human rebellion. In each changing generation, the one unchanging reality is God's steadfast love and never-failing fidelty.

After many years of wandering in the wilderness, the next generation of the Israelites was finally given the promised land. It was Joshua who led the conquest of Canaan where they settled in twelve tribes, named after the twelve sons of Jacob, who was Abraham's grandson. This was long before the day when King David would conquer Jerusalem and make it his capital city, and the glory days of King Solomon were, at this point, an undreamt-of fairy tale. Far from being a world power, Israel was a simple, constantly vulnerable confederacy of twelve tribes, loosely connected one to the other. There was no central government and no king because God was their King and Governor. In times of crisis, God's Spirit was poured out on an individual, making that person a judge—in biblical terms, a savior. The threat of an outside invasion was the common denominator in each of these instances. A foreign army would threaten the very survival of the tribes, and just when the future looked the bleakest, God would invariably raise up a judge to deliver them out of the hands of those who plundered them, and other tribes would then rally to preserve and protect their confederacy. The period of the judges continued for the first two hundred years in the land.

Not surprisingly, however, these years were not marked with single-minded fidelity to God. The history of this era, in fact, records a predictable cycle of faithfulness and apostasy. Just as the garden of Eden held the inherent perils of temptation and disobedience, so also did this new Eden, the promised land of Canaan. From their first days in the land, the Israelites lived alongside non-Israelite neighbors who worshiped different gods and were ever ready to lure the Israelites away from the one true God who had graciously delivered them from the yoke of Pharaoh. The Israelites repeatedly did what was evil in the sight of the Lord by abandoning the Lord and bowing down to the Canaanite gods. The command of the Lord was unambiguous in its claim: "You shall have no other gods before me." But the claim of God became an inconvenient impediment to the demands of carte blanche freedom, and, once again, human beings chose to live on their own terms rather than God's. The empty rituals of faith could not obscure the burning lust of the human heart for false gods that seemed immensely more relevant to the economic, social, and sexual pressures of the day. The Israelites were eager to enjoy the full measure of God's covenant love, but their hearts were stone cold when it came to offering the Lord their covenant faithfulness in return. God's anger repeatedly burned hot against the people, but God's character of unrelenting love and unshakable faithfulness prevailed, holding the tribal confederacy together.

Two hundred years after settling in the land, the Israelites found themselves at a great crossroads. Fiercely threatened by the menace of their enemies, especially the Philistines, they feared losing the promised land altogether. As they surveyed their enemies, they saw that the ones who were most to be feared had a king. Thus many of the Israelites began to fancy themselves after the pattern of foreign nations. Would they become like the other nations of the earth and have a king? Or would they remain as they always had been—ruled by the invisible Creator of the universe who had redeemed them from slavery and given them the land promised to Abraham? For many, it appeared to be only a question of political expedience, involving the judicious protection of military power and the deterrence of their enemies. But for others, this was supremely a spiritual juncture of faith, a time to acknowledge God as their one and only King and Governor, an occasion to confess the one true God in a world of competing claims. The biblical record is marked by great ambivalence concerning this decision, but it was a decision from which there would be no turning back. Finally, the Israelites demanded a king like the other kings of the earth. They wanted to be like the other nations with their brand of power and security in the politics of world affairs. A loose tribal confederacy they would no longer be. A modern state in a world of monarchs and thrones they would become.

Reluctantly and cautiously, God granted their request, and Saul was anointed king by the prophet Samuel. If the days of Saul were the first feeble steps toward the threshold of monarchy, the reigns of King David and King Solomon, during the tenth century B.C., ushered Israel across that threshold to the throne of power among the nations of the earth. King David made Jerusalem his capital city, and King Solomon built a temple where he anticipated the sovereign Lord of the universe would dwell and be worshiped and praised for all time to come. During the reigns of David and Solomon, Israel was changed from a loose tribal confederacy to a nation of security and power. Centuries after the implausible promise of land and progeny was first made to Abraham, not only were land and progeny living realities, but God promised that the throne of David would never lack an heir. As Israel finally became a world power, the eras of David and Solomon tell a story of remarkable splendor. The God who delivered the Israelites from the bonds of slavery and sustained them through their first tentative and ambivalent steps in the promised land now gave to Israel a bounteous world overflowing with goodness and prosperity. They had been rescued from the belly of death and given abundant life.

As they enjoyed the privileges of their new life, however, the human heart again burned with lust for false gods, and God's laws of love soon faded until they finally disappeared in the rubble of rebellion. God's claim on the life of Israel, unequivocal as it was, became community chaff to be thrown away and trampled under foot. The commandments of God became, in the people's hearts, an outdated faith now irrelevant in their sophisticated, pluralistic world. Moreover, their sins multiplied through economic injustice and heartless indifference to the needs of the weak and the plight of the poor. And as the spiritual decay of God's people took its toll, so also did the politics of national life. Infidelity had done its work, and the glory days were soon to vanish like a fleeting vapor. In the period following King Solomon, the nation became divided in civil dispute. For the duration, there would be not one Israel, but two—the Northern Kingdom, with its capital in Samaria, and the Southern Kingdom with its capital in Jerusalem.

It was a time of continuous rebellion against God. The covenant was now a quaint memory of a day once upon a time when God made half-forgotten promises to their ancestors. But it was all a misty, cloudy, distant memory. As the faith of Israel crumbled, so also did the monarchy, as Israel became thoroughly absorbed in the worship of foreign gods. Noah had been God's hope for a new beginning, but that hope had evaporated long ago. Abraham had been the seed of a nation that would be a living instrument in the hand of God to reclaim the entire creation, but now that expectation, too, was a fleeting wisp of wishful thinking. God had ushered a company of liberated slaves from their meager beginnings as a tribal confederacy to the world of kingdoms and empires, but they chose to take God's good gifts of love and squander them every one by whoring after false gods—more interesting gods, less demanding gods, gods that would give them life on their own terms, gods they could manipulate and control at will. Upon their arrival in the promised land, God's word had been unambiguously clear:

> Put away the gods that your ancestors served beyond the River and in Egypt, and serve the LORD . . . [and] choose this day whom you will serve. . . . If you forsake the LORD and serve foreign gods, then he will turn and do you harm, and consume you, after having done you good. (Josh. 24:14–20)

But the relished delights of forbidden fruit were more desirable than fidelity to the living God who had redeemed them from the misery of slavery.

The marvel, once again, was that God did not give up entirely but tenaciously hoped that the covenant community would return to its senses and that the earth would one day be filled with the consummate joy of all creation worshiping and serving God in ceaseless doxology. To that end, God sent the prophets to call the Israelites to repentance and faith. The prophets revealed not only the burning fire of divine wrath but also the heart-wrenching pathos of divine sorrow and anguish. Indeed, each page of the prophets' writings arose from the very soil of personal heartbreak that God suffered over the human family. Century after century, the prophets kept calling the covenant community to love God with all the heart and soul and might (Deut. 6:5) and to treat the neighbor with love and respect. In the midst of prosperity, they were to remember the poor of the earth and reach out to the stranger with hospitality and compassion. Above all, the Lord wanted the Israelites to live in joyful gratitude for divine grace and to repent of their sins by committing themselves anew to the knowledge and trust of God. This was the unrelenting message of redemption from the mouth of Elijah and Isaiah and Jeremiah and Hosea and Amos and Micah and all the other prophets. They kept calling, tirelessly calling with the saving purpose of God. Time and time again, their message of God's judgment was one of unflinching hope that all was not lost. Each time they spoke, God mercifully opened a window into the future. The loving purpose of God's judgment was to purge the covenant community of sin, to restore the joy of life under God's rule, and to begin anew in faith and obedience. Even as the Israelites raced toward self-destruction, God promised through the prophets that, if the covenant people would only repent of their sins and return to the Lord their God, mercy would be given. They would discover a cup running over with forgiving love, and they would most assuredly be saved from the advancing throes of destruction. God exercised judgment only as an instrument of love. Its purpose was to purge, to renew, to heal, and to restore.

But, once again, the covenant community wanted no part of the abundant life God had in mind. Repentance, turning from the service of self toward the service of God, is a costly act because it means self-surrender. As the once-mighty kingdom of Israel crumbled and fell, exile became God's judgment on a spiritually bankrupt and broken people. In approximately 722 B.C., the Northern Kingdom fell to the Assyrians, and in about 587 B.C., the last vestiges of the Southern Kingdom fell to Babylon. In the years following, the Israelites, once again landless and enslaved to foreign kings, wept bitter tears of regret by the waters of Babylon. "How could we sing the LORD's song in a foreign land?" (Ps. 137:4) they cried out in despair. But, miracle of miracles, God still was not finished with the covenant community. God's dream of reclaiming the whole of a lost creation was far from over because great is God's faithfulness. Even as the Israelites languished in exile, God raised up the prophet Isaiah (cf. 40–55) who announced to the feeble deportees that God had accepted their penance and was poised to gather the flock of Israel with infinite tenderness and lead them safely home again. Their sins would be forgiven, and the dawn of God's future would break forth upon them with glorious light. During this time, the memory that God had promised an everlasting kingdom was fueled by the precious hope that God would send a messiah to occupy the throne of David. He would be God's Anointed One to heal and redeem God's people, as human history advanced toward the new creation of God's love.

As power on the horizon of world events began to shift dramatically, Babylon fell to Cyrus of Persia, and in approximately 538 B.C., Cyrus set the Israelites free to return to Jerusalem. Some of them did return, but, to their great dismay, they returned to a Jerusalem in shambles. It was not as anyone remembered. The Temple lay in ruins, and the returning exiles faced the formidable challenges of rebuilding the great capital city of King David. But the glory days never returned and the rebirth of Israel as a major player in the halls of government simply did not materialize. In fact, Israel remained during those years a subprovince of the Persian empire.

As the centuries passed, it did seem as though God had spoken the final word on the subject of creation and the human experiment had been pronounced a miserable failure. The promises of God were now strangely silent. The promised land was irredeemably lost. The hope of the future was utterly spent. God's covenant had failed to produce a relationship of mutual love and trust, as had the gift of the promised land, the monarchy, and the passionate warnings of the prophets. So what would be God's disposition of the world once pronounced "very good"? Was the dream of God to use Israel in reclaiming the whole of creation now only a vanishing hope? And what would become of God's promise that the throne of David would last forever? Would God finally give up on the human family, or would God remain faithful?

The answer comes in the mightiest of all the mighty acts of God. Despite all the dishonor the human race had heaped on its relationship with God, and despite every act of obstinate rebellion, God still yearned to be loved, freely and joyously, by the human family. So God would now personally come to earth as a human being to dig us out of the rubble of our self-destruction and make us whole again.

In the fullness of time—more than five hundred years after the fall of the Southern Kingdom, as the Jews were nothing more than loathed and lowly subjects of Roman oppression—God became a tiny seed in the womb of a young peasant girl named Mary, who was betrothed to a man named Joseph, a descendent of King David. When the time came, in the way of humans, the Lord of the universe was delivered as a struggling, human baby into this world of sin and laid in a feeding trough in a stable in Bethlehem. The God who in the beginning had reached into the vast and empty chaos of nothingness and brought beauty and love to life became a finite human being in Jesus of Nazareth. As incomprehensible as it is, the timeless and eternal God personally entered the world of time and space. God would now personally empower the human family to live in covenant faithfulness, to love one another, and to exercise justice among neighbors. All the goodness and love, all the riches of abundant life that God had willed for Israel were now present in Jesus Christ. Jesus was the new Adam who would live the life of perfect obedience that God had intended in the first place. He was nothing less than "the image of the invisible God" (Col. 1:15).

But the human family, indeed an obstinate lot, decided to kill both the message and the messenger, because the Jesus God sent was not the Jesus anybody wanted. He came preaching and teaching in the name of a God whom the religious establishment could neither control nor manipulate, and that is a very dangerous kind of preaching and teaching. The people wanted a messiah who, like King David, would establish a political kingdom. They wanted the Romans kicked in the teeth, and they wanted God to deliver them once again to the world of prosperity and privilege. In short, they demanded a messiah who would restore them to the glory days of Israel's golden past, and any so-called messiah who failed to share that vision was obviously not of God. Instead of establishing a political kingdom, Jesus embodied a spiritual kingdom—a kingdom of compassion for the neighbor, of hospitality for the stranger, of neighborliness for and acceptance of those who were different, of sacrifice for the sake of others, of turning the other cheek in the midst of insult, of forgiving one's enemies seventy times seven (which was shorthand for saying, "as often as it takes to get the job done"), of caring for the poor and dispossessed, of loving God with all the heart and soul and mind and strength and the neighbor as the self. But make no mistake, this is not what they wanted.

Furthermore, this so-called Messiah befriended all the wrong kinds of people—sinners and tax collectors and prostitutes and every "untouchable" you can imagine. In fact, he was a known friend of every kind of social outcast whom good religious people hated. What's more, he made disciples not out of the community's most prominent people but out of a ragtag bunch of nobodies. And he did all of this in the name of God and as the act of God! It was utter blasphemy! This could not possibly be the Messiah, because he failed to live up to the people's expectations. They wanted a Savior who would make them prosperous, not expect too much in return, wink at their bigotry, and look the other way as they pursued their niggling fights for prominence. Instead, God sent a messiah who shattered every aspect of petty provincialism and defined the neighbor as all people, regardless of race or ethnicity or social class or gender or education or economic status or the myriad other distinctions that we humans delight in drawing. While he unfailingly honored the faith of his ancestors, Jesus condemned every aspect of conventional religion that was self-serving, and called all human beings to true repentance: turning *from* self-destruction *to* the justice and love of God.

This, however, is never a very palatable proposition for a human race hellbent on freedom without limits. So when they had heard quite enough repentance and the denial of self in the service of others, they lynched the Messiah. The religious authorities trumped up charges against him, condemned him to death, and then handed him over to the Roman officials who conveniently complied. Jesus was tried for treason, pronounced guilty, and sentenced to death. They then nailed him to a cross where he died a convicted felon between two common criminals.

Once more, it seemed as though God's love affair with the human family was finally over. After all, hadn't it ended in pathetic failure? The Messiah was dead. All hope was lost. God's love had been conquered by the vast, malignant chaos of human evil. But God was not finished. On the third day after Jesus was crucified, God raised him from the dead. No one knows how it happened. In the nearly two thousand years since the resurrection, scholars have written more pages in more books than can be counted, but no one has ever explained it. All we know is that Jesus Christ, who was dead as dead can be, was raised by the power of God and lived again; and because he lives, we too shall live. By the power of the one true God, Jesus Christ rose from the grave the triumphant Victor over everything that destroys our relationship with God and one another. From this time forward, every generation would know that nothing has the power to conquer God's love for us in Jesus Christ. Nothing in all creation, not even the deathly evil that has turned this world inside out and finally crucified the Savior of the world, has the power to stand between God and the human family. Despite every attempt to squander God's love and become our own gods, the Word of God contains a perpetual melody that has not and will not be silenced: Even when we are totally faithless, God remains faithful.

After the resurrection on Easter morning, Jesus appeared to his disciples and to other witnesses before ascending into heaven. He had promised, however, never to abandon his disciples and, on the day of Pentecost (cf. Acts 2), the Holy Spirit burst upon the disciple community with the power of God, giving birth to the church and sending forth the followers of the risen Christ to preach the gospel to the ends of the earth. Ever since the lives of those first believers were touched by grace, Christians all over the world for two thousand years have gladly announced the good news: "Christ is risen! He is risen indeed! Alleluia!" Because Jesus Christ lived and died and rose from the grave, we have the privilege of proclaiming the good news: "For God so loved the world that he gave his only Son, so that everyone who believes in him may not perish but may have eternal life" (John 3:16).

While you and I are able only to glimpse the power and glory of God in our earthly lives, the New Testament assures us that God is not through with this world. Even though Jesus is no longer physically with us, his Spirit rules over all. And because we know this is true, we are confident that evil no longer has the final word over us. *God* has the final word, and it is not a word of condemnation but of infinite love, of boundless mercy, of abundant and everlasting life. By the power of the crucified and risen Jesus Christ,

> God is working His purpose out as year succeeds to year:
> God is working His purpose out, and the time is drawing near;
> Nearer and nearer draws the time, the time that shall surely be,
> When the earth shall be filled with the glory of God
> As the waters cover the sea.[6]

Nothing will stop the Lord of all creation. God's love is eternal. God's judgment is perfect. God's mercy is sure. God's power is sovereign. Great is God's faithfulness. The kingdom and the power and the glory belong to God forever and ever!

A Common Memory:
The Bible as Our Personal Story

That is the story of our faith—the old, old story of Jesus and his love that Christians have the joy of telling in word and deed. The story of the Bible, however, is not just the saga of people who lived in long ago times and places. It also is *our* story, the saga of *our* days and weeks and months and years. The scriptures present us with a peculiar genealogy—*our own*!

> When your children ask you in time to come, "What is the meaning of the decrees and the statutes and the ordinances that the LORD our God has commanded you?" then you shall say to your children, "We were Pharaoh's slaves in Egypt, but the LORD brought us out of Egypt with a mighty hand." (Deut. 6:20–21)

In a sermon several years ago, I attempted to make this very point, using this passage from Deuteronomy to suggest that, in passing the story of the Bible from generation to generation, we are in essence teaching our children their family tree. In particular, I said that our children need to know that *we* were once slaves of Pharaoh in Egypt, but the Lord heard *our* cries of anguish and brought *us* out of Egypt with a mighty hand. It is for this very reason that we sing:

> Were you there when they crucified my Lord?
> . . . .
> Where you there when they nailed him to the tree?
> . . . .
> Were you there when they pierced him in the side?
> . . . .
> Were you there when they laid him in the tomb?[7]

The implicit answer is, "Yes, indeed!" The story of the crucifixion is not just the story of those who physically strung Jesus up and left him to die, but is the story of *my* guilt and *my* need for redemption. After the sermon, I was approached by a member of the congregation who said that this was a new idea for her, that she had never thought of the characters and events of the Bible in such graphically personal terms.

My hunch is that this is true for many of us. We have learned through the years to keep the Bible at arm's length, believing it to be mainly about ancient times and places lost long ago in the rubble of history. But the Bible is as contemporary as it is ancient. In reading about Adam and Eve in the garden of Eden (Gen. 1–3), we peer into a mirror. In hearing the story of Cain and Abel

(Gen. 4), we see a portrait of our own petty rivalries to be "Number One" no matter who gets hurt in the process. In looking in on David and Bathsheba in the midst of their sordid afternoon fling between the sheets and David's subsequent plot to have his mistress's husband, Uriah the Hittite, killed in battle (2 Sam. 11-12), we are given a glimpse into our own sordid, grasping ways, and our personal penchant for the seedy when we think no one is looking. The same is true of the story of Moses and Joshua and Samuel and all the prophets, and of Peter and James and John and Mary and Martha and Paul. In the midst of the story, we come to see that we are related; these are *our* fathers and mothers, *our* sisters and brothers. As John H. Leith has reminded us, our life stories are not primarily a matter of biological heritage; they are a spiritual heritage given to us through a common memory.[8]

We tell the old, old story because of its inherent power to connect us to the community of God in all times and places, and because it contains the very "stuff" of our lives—*our* hopes and fears, *our* betrayals and denials, *our* petty differences, *our* repentance, *our* self-surrender, *our* quest for genuine human community, *our* redemption in Jesus Christ, *our* victory over death given by the love of the cross and the power of the empty tomb, *our* uncommon courage inspired by the daily presence of the risen Christ, *our* personal sacrifices given for the sake of following Christ. By and through this story, persons of radically diverse backgrounds—whether they be social or familial or economic or racial or national or ethnic—are given a common memory of faith and find themselves, by a sheer miracle of God's grace, joining hands and hearts and voices in the service of Jesus Christ. This is our only hope for renewal: a miracle of God, empowering congregations to respond anew with courageous obedience and joyful trust in the One who died on the cross and rose from the grave.

We turn now to some of the seeds of our common memory found in the story of the Bible. Here is both challenge and comfort for the trials of today. Here is hope for the future to which God calls us.

Truth 1

God Is in Charge

> *To whom then will you compare me,*
>> *or who is my equal? says the Holy One. . . .*
> *Have you not known? Have you not heard?*
> *The LORD is the everlasting God,*
>> *the Creator of the ends of the earth.*

(Isa. 40:25, 28a)

Beginning with God

With the story of the Bible as our foundation for wrestling with the reality of God, we come now to the soaring melody to which the symphony of scripture untiringly returns—*the sovereignty of God*. To speak of God's sovereignty is to confess unequivocally that, despite abundant evidence to the contrary, *God is in charge*.

"O Lord, our Sovereign, how majestic is your name in all the earth!" (Psalm 8) sings the psalmist. The all-powerful God who spoke the universe into existence is the sovereign Lord "who has measured the waters in the hollow of his hand and marked off the heavens with a span," the One before whom "all the nations are as nothing":

> Have you not known? Have you not heard?
> . . . .
> It is he [the LORD] who sits above the circle of the earth,
>> and its inhabitants are like grasshoppers;
> who stretches out the heavens like a curtain,
>> and spreads them like a tent to live in;
> who brings princes to naught,
>> and makes the rulers of the earth as nothing.

(Isa. 40:21–23)

And this is the same God of whom generations of Christians have sung with triumphant gladness: "The kingdom of the world has become the kingdom of our Lord and of his Christ, and he will reign forever and ever" (Rev. 11:15).

Reformed theology begins on a note of supreme joy: the praise and majesty of the sovereign God of all creation. But much hangs on how we define the word "sovereignty." First, consider what we do *not* mean when we say that God is in charge.

Confusing God's Power
with Fatalism and Brute Force

I remember making a pastoral call one evening on a family who had just suffered a terrible tragedy. One always feels inadequate in such a situation, yet I have learned through the years that my job in that setting is simply to be there with the heart of a pastor, to focus on the promises of God in scripture, and to offer prayer for a discernable experience of God's presence in the midnight madness of despair. Sometimes, however, I run into people who instantly feel the need to sort out theologically the tragedy that has just ripped through their lives. And more often than not, they attempt to do so by appealing to their understanding of the sovereignty of God. They don't ordinarily use those words—sovereignty of God—but that's what they mean. On this particular occasion, the darkness of night was no match for the black hole of pain inside the home of this particular parishioner. "You know, Steve, this simply was the will of God; that's all I can make of it," he said as a river of tears began to flow. At other times, I have heard parishioners try to justify the crushing blow they have suffered with a stoic, stiff upper lip: "I don't understand why this had to happen. It seems so unfair. But God knows what he's doing, so I just have to accept it." When this happens, I want to ask, "Why do you think God's hand is on the trigger of every tragedy? Isn't it possible that this heartbreak that has come crashing into your life *isn't* the will of God?" Yet I am aware that people sometimes implicate God in their suffering because they desperately need to see a connection between the despair they face and the God in whom they trust, and it is far better for God to be implicated than uninvolved.

A frequent variation on this misunderstanding of the sovereignty of God is the notion that Presbyterianism is synonymous with a fatalism over which we have absolutely no control. I remember a conversation with another parishioner during my early years as a pastor. I hadn't been out of seminary too awfully long and was still laboring under the mistaken assumption that God had appointed me personally to take on the world *and* straighten out the church, and that I, in fact, was poised to accomplish what pastors had been unable to do for twenty unendurably long centuries. This parishioner's story was sad indeed. He had been widowed early in life and left by himself to raise a son whom he loved better than life itself. There he was trying to raise a teenage boy as a single parent in a changing world, and life was anything but easy. But he said to me one day, "I know this is God's will, and I can accept it because I'm a good Presbyterian who knows that whatever will be will be." And I still remember how he emphasized that last part: *whatever will be will be.* Somehow the rigors of academic study at the seminary had not prepared me to deal with a well-meaning parishioner who thought that "Que Sera, Sera" was the theme song of the Presbyterian Church, as if our lives amount to nothing more than the playing out of an intractable script over which we have neither choice nor control.

In no way do I mean to belittle the beliefs of these parishioners. They were well-meaning in every way, utterly devoted to the church and, even more important, were trying to make sense of the woeful hand they had been dealt in the light of their faith in Jesus Christ. But they help us to see ourselves in the mirror of their struggles, and they nudge us to think more clearly about what the sovereignty of God means in the agonizing heartbreak of life. What, after all, do we mean when we say that God is all-powerful? Is the power of God the same thing as brute force? Does faith in God equal a resigned fatalism that makes God personally responsible for everything that happens in the world and consigns you and me to the role of mere puppets on God's cosmic string? Does God set the ravages of natural disaster and personal calamity by divine decree? And does the sovereignty of God mean that, if something bad happens to us, then it must be because God wanted it to happen?

Precisely at the point of answering such questions, the Reformed tradition has not always been helpful. Many of our traditional Reformed beliefs on this subject were inherited from scholastic medieval theology and became commonplace in our heritage.[1] The Westminster Confession of Faith, for example, says that "God from all eternity did, by the most wise and holy counsel of his own will, freely and unchangeably ordain whatsoever comes to pass."[2] Calvin himself declared that we "are governed by God's secret plan in such a way that nothing happens except what is knowingly and willingly decreed by him," and "in times of adversity believers comfort themselves with the solace that they suffer nothing except by God's ordinance and command, for they are under his hand."[3] And if that isn't enough to implicate God as the origin of every misfortune in the universe, Calvin goes so far as to say that "some mothers have full and abundant breasts, but others' are almost dry, as God wills to feed one more liberally, but another more meagerly."[4]

But is this the loving providence of the sovereign God revealed in scripture? The God whose heart was utterly broken with grief over the rebellion of the human race? Is this the loving providence of the Sovereign One who chose out of love to enter the womb of a young peasant girl named Mary and become human in Jesus of Nazareth? And are we honestly to believe that "every success is God's blessing, and calamity and adversity his curse"?[5]

Indeed not. The sovereignty of God does not reduce human life to a narrow determinism in which God's power is synonymous with the arbitrary exercise of brute force. God is not an all-powerful tyrant who capriciously dishes out blessings and curses by divine whim. As Professor Shirley Guthrie has suggested, "If we are to be faithful to Scripture and to formulate a theology relevant for our time, we cannot abandon the traditional Reformed emphasis on God's honor, glory, majesty, and sovereign power,"[6] yet we must avoid "a fatalistic determinism that makes God directly or indirectly responsible for every bad as well as good thing that happens in the world and demands that pious Christians accept whatever happens to them, their loved ones, and everyone else as 'the will of God': health *and* sickness, success *and* failure, life *and* death, good *and* evil."[7] Indeed, God is not a Cosmic Sadist. The words, *sovereignty of God*, must surely point in another direction.

Some of my fondest memories of Sunday evening worship services as a child are of singing hymns written specifically for the evening, and "The Day Thou Gavest, Lord, Is Ended" was one we sang often. This beautiful hymn culminates with a daring declaration as the uncertainties of the darkness arrive and we acknowledge the eternal hand that holds and protects us:

> So be it, Lord; Thy throne shall never,
> Like earth's proud empires, pass away;
> Thy kingdom stands, and grows for ever
> Till all Thy creatures own thy sway.[8]

But what is the nature of God's kingdom? What kind of sovereignty is it that will never pass away?

The Peculiar Power of God

The question of God's sovereignty is one that gnaws at our souls in the harrowing agonies of life. Everywhere we look, it seems, there is unbearable pain in the world, not to mention the anguish inside our own skin. If God is truly in charge of the world, then why is there so much suffering? If God is indeed sovereign, then why must we face the tragedies of disease and heartbreak, the ravages of bigotry and pride? Why are there still children around the globe whose swollen bellies tell a story too painful for words? And why doesn't God bring an end to the hatred of ethnic cleansing, as well as the crushing grief of broken homes and shattered dreams? When I see the evening news, sometimes all I can think is, "Why doesn't God use all the power of heaven to end the pain and anguish that we humans hurl at one another?" As Robert Farrar Capon has pointed out, theoretically, of course, God has all the power needed to do just that. But such theorizing is not the way the Bible approaches the subject of God's sovereignty;[9] this is not the way God has chosen to act. And just now we have come to the sticky issue of the difference between God's power and human power.

Human beings know a great deal about power, especially what Capon calls the straight-line brand of power[10] that works by external force. The wielding of power by intimidation and threat is commonplace among the movers and shakers of this world. That kind of power gets the job done; it produces results. We know, for example, how to send a bomb from one part of the planet to another and blow our so-called enemies to smithereens. That is power—raw, concentrated power—and it works. Indeed, from the dawn of civilization, human history has been splattered with the blood of that kind of power. Likewise, we know all about wielding straight-line power closer to home. It happens every day as people bully their way around the office or threaten their way around the school or bulldoze the rest of the family toward a desired end.

But this is not how God is. The power of God is a peculiar power, because it is not the power of coercion. It is not brute force. God does not rule by fiat, or by browbeating and bulldozing people into action. No, God is not a Celestial Bully who proves divine sovereignty by external force. Quite to the contrary, says Capon, the power of God is paradoxical power. It "looks for all the world like weakness,"[11] because it is the sovereignty of divine love. Frederick Buechner says it this way:

> So the power of God stands in violent contrast with the power of [human beings]. It is not external like [human] power, but internal. By applying external pressure, I can make a person do what I want him to do. This is [human] power. But as for making him be what I want him to be, without at the same time destroying his freedom, only love can make this happen. And love makes it happen not coercively, but by creating a situation in which, of our own free will, we want to be what love wants us to be. And because God's love is uncoercive and treasures our freedom—if above all he wants us to love him, then we must be left free not to love him—we are free to resist it, deny it, crucify it finally, which we do again and again. This is our terrible freedom, which love refuses to overpower so that, in this, the greatest of all powers, God's power, is itself powerless.[12]

Because we encounter God's peculiar power most clearly in Jesus Christ, we turn now to the outpouring of God's sovereign love in him.

The Sovereign God Whom
We Know in Jesus Christ

The sovereign Lord whose kingdom lasts forever is none other than the God who is revealed in the person and work of Jesus Christ. "He is the image of the invisible God" (Col. 1:15). We see God's face in the face of Jesus Christ, and we experience the nature and character of God as Jesus Christ is nailed to the cross where he endures the ultimate brutality of human hatred. The birth, ministry, death, and resurrection of Jesus Christ reveal that the peculiar sovereignty of God is not the capricious wielding of brute force but the holy passion of suffering love. The reigning Monarch of all creation is also the humble Servant who embodies divine love. Karl Barth has explained it with these words:

> God's deity is thus no prison in which He can exist only in and for Himself.
> It is rather His freedom to be in and for Himself but also with and for us, to
> assert but also to sacrifice Himself, to be wholly exalted but also completely
> humble, not only almighty but also almighty mercy, not only Lord but also
> servant, not only judge but also Himself the judged, not only man's eternal
> king but also his brother in time.[13]

The sovereignty of God is the sovereignty of love. It is the living, eternal power of the One who is "not only almighty but also almighty mercy," the One whom we encounter in Jesus Christ.

At this point, we need to pay close attention to the content of the gospel, for here we meet the core conviction that *divine revelation* stands at the center of the Christian faith. We do not define God. Rather, God defines himself. The nature of God is a *revealed* nature. The love of God reaching out to judge, to purge, to heal, and to save is a *revealed* love. The Christian faith has not been spun from the hopes and dreams of human imagination, and neither is it our best estimation of what we need out of an even-handed religion. That kind of religion is extremely convenient and serviceable. But it is not what God has given us and has absolutely nothing to do with the faith to which God calls us. We do not come to know God by imagining who God might be, could be, or should be, were God to act according to our best ideas of God. Rather, we come to know God *only as God chooses to be revealed.* And the sovereign Lord of all creation is the God who reveals himself as a helpless, vulnerable, wailing, mortal baby in Jesus of Nazareth, who was laid in a common cattle trough for a crib. This Jesus was King of Kings and Lord of Lords, yet he found a home not in a palace or the halls of government or among the rich and famous, but in the lives of common, ordinary sinners, many of whom were despised by the keepers of straight-line power. Jesus showed us that the power of heaven's eternal King is supremely the power "to bring good news to the poor . . . to proclaim release to the captives and the recovery of sight to the blind, to let the oppressed go free, and to proclaim the year of the Lord's favor" (Luke 4:18–19). And this God whom we call Lord is the very one who was executed as a convicted felon on a cross of Roman justice, having provoked the wrath of mainline religious leaders by challenging their faith as shallow and vapid and piously self-serving. Yes, the God who is in charge is the long-awaited Messiah who was stripped, beaten, spat on by hate-filled, mocking executioners, and nailed to the cross as he cried out in agonizing despair, "My God, my God, why have you forsaken me?" (Matt. 27:46; Mark 15:34). And the sovereign Lord of all creation is the Victor who rose from the dead on Easter morning and appeared to his disciples in risen power. Because Christ lives, we too shall live, and nothing in all creation will finally have the power to separate us from the love God has given us in Jesus Christ.

That is the sovereignty of God. That is the peculiar power revealed in the vulnerability and apparent weakness of divine love. This is the sovereignty of a love so high, so wide, and so deep that it willingly suffers even to the point of sacrifice for the sake of the beloved and, in doing so, triumphs over all the powers of destruction. "For God so *loved* the world that he gave his only Son" (John 3:16; italics added here and below). "We love because *he first loved us*" (1 John 4:19). "See what *love* the Father has given us, that we should be called children of God" (1 John 3:1). "But God proves his *love* for us in that while we were still sinners Christ died for us" (Rom. 5:8). The sovereignty of God is not the capricious wielding of brute force but the sacrifice of love. If you want to know the sovereignty of God, then look at the cross of Jesus Christ; there it is in all its heart-wrenching glory. "Veiled in flesh the God-head see,"[14] we sing as the purple mood of Advent gives way to the brilliant joy of Christmas, and "Word of the Father, now in flesh appearing!"[15] The God revealed on the cross of Jesus Christ is the almighty God who is *almighty mercy*, and whose peculiar sovereignty can only be known and experienced in divine vulnerability.

> God's high freedom in Jesus Christ is His freedom for *love*. The divine capacity . . . is manifestly also God's capacity to bend downwards, to attach Himself to another and this other to Himself.[16]

None of our lives are perfect; we all have our demons. Not a week goes by that the daily news fails to bring into our living rooms the glut of hatred and warfare and suffering and strife that wreak havoc in every part of the globe. In every land and nation, the blood of brothers and sisters spilled at the hands of human hatred cries out the ghastly abominations of our inhumanity against each other. Then we wake up one morning to discover that terrorists have hijacked and intentionally flown jumbo jets into both towers of the World Trade Center in New York City and into the Pentagon in the nation's capital, leaving behind untold death and destruction and devastation as visible signs of horrific hate. Closer to home, marriages that we once thought were made in heaven break up. Cancer or some other dreaded disease rips through a family's life. And the workplace, it seems, is never quite what anyone hoped it would be—unexpected strife, unfulfilled expectations, unneeded envy, unwanted friction. Even the church is bedeviled by warring factions, dominated at times by misguided leaders, and always struggling to bear witness to the divine in a society that is human to the core. In such a world as this, if we believe that the sovereign power of God is synonymous with brute force, then we have two unhappy choices. Either God is on the side of the enemy, clearly wielding brute force to the detriment of the human family, or else God is a distant and indifferent deity who is fully able to intervene in the devastations of life but doesn't. The gospel, thankfully, takes us to neither of these conclusions. *The God who is revealed in Jesus Christ is the God whose sovereign power is supremely seen in the divine willingness "to bend downwards, to attach Himself to another and this other to Himself."* The sovereign Lord of all creation is also our human brother, Jesus Christ, who meets us in the black hole of depression and despair, in the death-filled rubble of smoldering buildings, in the agony of cracked relationships, in the turmoil of parenthood, in the turbulence of adolescence, in the struggle to find a vocation in life, in the infirmities of aging, in the heart's desire to be faithful to God and, finally, in the valley of the shadow of death. And because our God is willing to "bend downwards," we sing with joy:

> Praise, my soul, the King of heaven;
> To His feet thy tribute bring;
> Ransomed, healed, restored, forgiven,
> Evermore His praises sing: Alleluia! Alleluia!
> Praise the everlasting King.[17]

Where, Then, Is God
When Life Hurts So Much?

Shortly after William Sloane Coffin's son, Alex, was tragically killed in an automobile accident, Coffin preached a sermon in which he addressed some of these very issues. His treatment of what is and is not the will of God is all the more poignant and moving because it comes from the bowels of his own despair:

When a person dies, there are many things that can be said, and there is at least one thing that should never be said. The night after Alex died I was sitting in the living room of my sister's house outside of Boston, when the front door opened and in came a nice-looking middle-aged woman, carrying about eighteen quiches. When she saw me she shook her head, then headed for the kitchen, saying sadly over her shoulder, "I just don't understand the will of God." Instantly I was up and in hot pursuit, swarming all over her. "I'll say you don't, lady!" I said. . . . "Do you think it was the will of God that Alex never fixed that lousy windshield wiper of his, that he was probably driving too fast in such a storm, that he probably had had a couple of 'frosties' too many? Do you think it is God's will that there are no streetlights along that stretch of road, and no guard rail separating the road and Boston Harbor?"

For some reason, nothing so infuriates me as the incapacity of seemingly intelligent people to get it through their heads that God doesn't go around this world with his finger on triggers, his fist around knives, his hands on steering wheels. God is dead set against all unnatural deaths. And Christ spent an inordinate amount of time delivering people from paralysis, insanity, leprosy, and muteness. . . . The one thing that should never be said when someone dies is "It is the will of God." Never do we know enough to say that. My own consolation lies in knowing that it was *not* the will of God that Alex die; that when the waves closed over the sinking car, God's heart was the first of all our hearts to break.[18]

These words, straight from the pieces of a broken heart, offer an immensely comforting perspective on human tragedy and suffering. Indeed, God's finger is not on the trigger of every tragedy. Jesus said, "I came that they may have life, and have it abundantly" (John 10:10b). God wills goodness for our lives, not tragedy, not despair. But the theology of "God's finger is not on the trigger of every tragedy" holds its own brand of danger. The danger is that we will come to believe that there are things that happen in the world over which God is *not* sovereign, that there are some things in our lives that simply are so horrific that they lie beyond the scope of God's sovereign power and love. But precisely at this point, the faith of the Bible makes one of its most daring assertions. There is a great deal about God that we do not understand, and never will in this lifetime. Indeed, there is much about tragedy and suffering that the human mind will never comprehend. And try as we might, the sovereignty of God refuses to be reduced to a doctrine that presumes to have "figured out" everything we want to know about God's peculiar power. *But the one thing we know for sure is this: Because of the cross and resurrection of Jesus Christ, there is no horror so great that God cannot be at work in it. There is no terror that God cannot bend to God's good purposes.*

God Overrules Our Evil for Good

In Genesis 37–50, the story of Joseph and his brothers shows us the sovereign power of God to bend even our evil deeds to the goodness of divine purpose. Joseph is a lad of seventeen, and his brothers hate him with such a passion that they literally want him dead. It is perfectly obvious to everyone that Joseph, the son of Jacob's old age, is Daddy's pampered pet, and you know how the pampered pets of this world are resented. Joseph is the one who gets all of Daddy's special favors. Among the most prized of Jacob's gifts to Joseph is a long robe with sleeves, a symbol of status and prestige and parental favor with which the others were not graced. But what truly provokes the brothers' wrath are the dreams that Joseph has, dreams in which Joseph reigns over his entire family—mother, father, and brothers all.

One day, Joseph's brothers are out pasturing their father's flock, and Jacob sends Joseph to check on them. As Joseph approaches, the plot thickens with a malice dark enough for murder. His brothers see him coming from a distance, and their hearts are racked with jealousy and hate. Here comes Daddy's favorite! Here comes the spoiled brat who gets all the fancy clothes and gets to stay at home while we work in the stinking field! Yes, here comes Daddy's baby, Daddy's favorite, Daddy's precious! And suddenly the brothers' anger turns to rage, and they decide to do away with little brother once and for all.

By now, Joseph is almost there, and Plan A quickly gels. They decide to kill him and throw him into a pit, then go home and tell dear old Dad that, alas, a wild animal devoured his favorite son. On second thought, however, they decide not to take his life. So they throw him into a pit while they eat their lunch and contemplate Plan B. As good fortune would have it, a caravan of traders en route to Egypt passes by, so the brothers lift Joseph out of the pit and sell him to the traders for twenty pieces of silver. With Joseph on his way to Egypt, his brothers slaughter a goat, dip Joseph's robe in the goat's blood, and go home with long faces to announce the untimely demise of baby brother. Jacob is beside himself with grief, certain that Joseph is dead.

In the coming years, Joseph's ability as an interpreter of dreams commands the Egyptian Pharaoh's notice. In fact, because of Joseph's interpretation of Pharaoh's dreams, the Egyptians are warned of an approaching famine. Joseph says that there will be seven plenteous years of harvest prior to the famine, so his advice is to store as much food as possible during those seven years in order to have an abundance in reserve during the years of famine. Joseph's proposal pleases Pharaoh so much that Joseph is made prime minister of Egypt, second only to Pharaoh himself.

After the seven years of abundant harvest, the famine hits just as Joseph had predicted. And back home, Jacob and the rest of the family are hungry. Jacob learns, however, that there is grain in Egypt, so he sends his sons to purchase some, which brings them face to face with the brother they had sold into slavery thirteen years earlier. While the brothers do not recognize Joseph, he without a doubt recognizes them. One would expect Joseph's wrath to be poured out with unrestrained vengeance on his brothers. Yet just then the story moves to a gracious end, as Joseph treats his brothers with utmost generosity and kindness. He says to them,

> "I am your brother, Joseph, whom you sold into Egypt. And now do not be distressed, or angry with yourself, because you sold me here; for God sent me before you to preserve life. . . . God sent me before you to preserve for you a remnant on earth, and to keep alive for you many survivors. So it was not you who sent me here, but God." (Gen. 45:4b–5, 7–8a)

It is a bold and moving moment in the biblical story. "It was not you who sent me here, but God." The victim of a hate-filled crime attributes the crime to God's promise keeping, God's providence, God's sovereignty in working through the evil in our world.

After a happy reunion between Joseph and his brothers, the entire family comes to Egypt and is saved from the famine. At the death of Jacob, however, the brothers fear for their lives. Without Dad to intercede for them, what will Joseph do to the ones who had once hated him enough to sell him into slavery? Surely he will now do the human thing and exact his revenge. Yet amazingly, Joseph again interprets everything that has happened within the larger scope of God's sovereign purpose:

> "Do not be afraid! Am I in the place of God? Even though you intended to do harm to me, God intended it for good, in order to preserve a numerous people, as he is doing today." (Gen. 50:19–20)

An earlier translation said it this way: "As for you, you meant evil against me; but God meant it for good . . ." (RSV). Biblical faith comes from the deep, abiding conviction that there is literally nothing in life so full of hate or so swollen with enmity that it is finally outside the sovereign power of God to redeem and bend to divine purpose. Christians, of course, read the story of Jacob and his loss, of Joseph and his tragedy, through the cross of Jesus Christ on which another Father gave up a Son, and another Son suffered the ultimate "tragedy" for the sins of the world. The good news of the gospel is that God is able and willing to take even the worst of human failure and rebellion and use it, work with it, redeem it. Such is the sovereignty of God's peculiar power. *Because of the cross and resurrection of Jesus Christ, there is no horror so great that God cannot be at work in it. There is no terror that God can-*

not bend to God's good purposes. As Paul says, "We know that all things work together for good for those who love God, who are called according to his purpose" (Rom. 8:28).

Some Practical Implications of the Sovereignty of God

If Christians believe that God is all-powerful, how does this conviction shape and govern our lives? What does the conviction that God is sovereign have to do with such things as living faithfully with a spouse, having babies, attending school, going to work, and living out one's faith in the life of the church? John Leith argues that "the central theme of Calvinist theology, which holds it all together, is the conviction that every human being has every moment to do with the living God,"[19] and that the practical implications of an emphasis on the sovereignty of God are clearly seen in the faithful life that flows from it.[20]

Disciples of Jesus Christ are called, in every situation of life, to raise the God question. Life would be quite different—would it not?—were we to believe deep down that the sovereign God wants to shape every moment of our lives. When we relate to our spouse, God is involved, whether in the living room or the bedroom. When we live in the constant fray of raising children, teaching them right from wrong and helping them to form a core character of moral integrity, God meets us there as well. When we are called on in our jobs to deal with difficult personalities, we are dealing not just with people who may irritate and annoy us but with the living God of all creation. When we find ourselves making ethical decisions or maintaining friendships or embarking on vocational choices, it is not just a matter of our personal preferences and desires but of the sovereign God who is in charge of our lives. That is to say, the question of God's sovereignty and the question of human faithfulness go hand in hand; sovereignty and service are but two sides of the same coin. So it is useless to pontificate about the high sovereignty of God apart from the concrete, everyday difference it makes in our lives because, if God is truly in charge of our lives, we will want with all our hearts to serve him. The Westminster Shorter Catechism begins by asking, "What is the chief end of human life?" And the answer is "to glorify God and to enjoy God forever."[21] Glorifying God *by participating in the purposes of God for the world*—that is the sovereignty of God in action.

This, however, is one of the hardest of all truths for a culture thoroughly saturated by the conviction that all significant discussion about life begins with me and my needs. The Bible teaches us to begin not with ourselves but with God; not with our tenuous plight in the jungle of life's uncertainties but with God's saving purpose for the entire cosmos; not with our hopes and dreams for a happy and trouble-free life that serves us everything we want and more on a silver platter but with God's sovereign power to create, redeem, and sustain life. In the words of John Leith,

> The theocentric [God-centered] character of Reformed faith sets it over against every ethic of self-realization, against inordinate concern with the salvation of one's own soul, against excessive preoccupation with questions of personal identity. The great fact is God, and the true vocation of every human being is trust in him and loyalty to his cause.[22]

As with most pastors, it is my responsibility every fall to teach officer training for our newly elected elders and deacons, and we usually begin the theological part of our classes with a discussion of how the ramifications of God's sovereignty cut against the grain of American culture. The children spawned by our culture grow up believing that the formative questions of life are, Will this enable me to get what I want out of life? Will it make my dreams come true? Will it make me comfortable and ever more prosperous? But on the other hand, those who believe that serving God is the very purpose for which we were born know deep down inside that our dreams are sometimes the wrong dreams. Maybe what I want to get out of life is not what God wants out of my life. And what if "comfortable" and "ever more prosperous" don't even make the list of what God wants for the community of Jesus Christ? Those who take the sovereignty of God seriously understand that the defining questions are very different: What is the will of *God* for my life? What does *God*, who created and redeemed me, want from me? What can I do in my marriage, in raising my children, in my job, in my civic responsibilities, and in my church that will honor and glorify *God*? When serving God becomes the central focus of one's life, priorities change and what once seemed supremely important no longer matters. I say again, We Christians are called, in every situation of life, to raise the God question.

This, of course, flies squarely in the face of everything near and dear to the American dream. "Go for the gusto!" is the mantra that bombards American children from their earliest moments in life, and they learn it not only from the slick savvy of Madison Avenue but also from the priorities they see their parents making. Life then becomes a never-ending exercise in doing what makes us feel good. Even the life of the church is often judged on the merits of whether or not it provides a feel-good experience and on the basis of what goods and services it provides for its members. One evening many years ago, I went to the home of a young man and woman who had been visiting our church and, therefore, had been sized up as hot prospects for church membership. Their first child was getting on toward the age when they thought she should be in Sunday school, so they were out "church shopping." After all the pleasantries were exchanged and they had served the obligatory glass of iced tea, they were ready to get down to business. "Tell us, Pastor, why should we join your church?" they wanted to know. "What does your congregation have to offer that the others in town do not?" I suddenly felt as though I were a salesperson in a shoe store and the "customer" was comparing various labels on display and asking me to rate and rank one brand over all the others. After a few ponderous moments of sizing up the situation, I answered as honestly as I knew how. "I think you should join our church," I said, "if you see it as a community that will empower you to serve Jesus Christ. The real issue is not what our congregation has to offer you, but how and in what context you see yourselves serving Jesus Christ." This was *not* the answer they wanted, and I remember being stared at momentarily as if I suddenly had sprouted a second head. The conversation did not last much longer, and we never saw or heard from them again.

I have often thought about that conversation, and there is a sense, of course, in which I wish I had handled it differently. The part of me that confuses faithfulness with success cringes at what I said to that couple. We wanted our church to grow, and I blew it. We wanted our congregation to be warm and friendly and welcoming and inviting, and I somehow let the convictions of my theology betray that intention. But I must say that, faced with the same question, I would answer today in exactly the same way because "How can I serve God?" is always the defining question, not "What can I get out of the church?" or "How will it make me feel about myself?"

A large part of our beleaguering biblical and theological amnesia is the failure to remember that the Bible and, therefore, the life of the Christian, is first and foremost *God's* story, not ours, and the charter of the church's life is *God's* agenda, not ours. Try picturing the decisions Abraham and Sarah had to make if their only concern was, "What's in it for us?" Can you imagine Moses charging toward the raging waters of the Red Sea with the army of Pharaoh in hot pursuit, thinking, "Hmm . . . let me see now; is this going to make all my dreams come true?" Or imagine Mary, the mother of Jesus, judging Gabriel's proposition about being pregnant out of wedlock on the merits of how it made her feel about herself in the context of her conservative neighborhood. And remember that, much to their consternation, Jesus repeatedly told his disciples that a relationship with him has absolutely nothing to do with milking God for all the goodies we can weasel out of him. Rather, the whole point from beginning to end is *serving God on God's terms.* "In the

New Testament," writes Karl Barth, "they did not come to the Church merely so that they might be saved and happy, but that they might have the signal privilege of serving the Lord."[23]

John Calvin lived out his theological convictions not in the ivory tower of academic life but as he preached and taught the gospel, catechized the children of the church, and executed the administrative duties of leading a congregation, not to mention those of civil and church politics. He struggled, just as we all do, to live out the call of God in the concrete realities of everyday life, and Calvin knew firsthand how difficult it is when one's personal desires and the will of God are at odds with each other. An illustration from Calvin's life aptly reveals the struggle within his soul as he wrestled with "the great fact" as the primary reality of his life. In 1541, Calvin faced a major decision. Would he remain in Strasbourg or return to Geneva? Although there was enormous pressure to return to Geneva, the desire of his heart was to remain in Strasbourg. Calvin, however, did not merely act on his personal preference but struggled instead to discern what God wanted out of his life, and he came to realize that God's will was for him to return to Geneva. Against his personal preferences, return to Geneva he did. Calvin's letter to his friend Farel, who had insisted that Calvin return to Geneva, reveals the struggle of his soul:

> As to my intended course of proceeding, this is my present feeling: had I the choice at my own disposal, nothing would be less agreeable to me than to follow your advice. But when I remember that I am not my own, I offer up my heart, presented as a sacrifice to the Lord. . . . And for myself, I protest that I have no other desire than that, setting aside all consideration of me, they may look only to what is most for the glory of God and the advantage of the Church. . . . I am well aware . . . that it is God with whom I have to do. . . . Therefore I submit my will and my affections, subdued and held-fast, to the obedience of God; and whenever I am at a loss for counsel of my own, I submit myself to those by whom I hope that the Lord himself will speak to me.[24]

Wrestling with God as "the great fact" of life is the lifelong vocation to which God calls us and is one concrete way of living out our deep conviction that God is sovereign. It is a matter of praying for God's will to be done in and through us. And while this is not the whole struggle by any stretch of the imagination, wanting God's will means realizing that our personal preferences may not be synonymous with the will of God, and discerning the difference between the two is a pure gift of God's grace. Along these lines, William Barclay has written a prayer that moves me each time I read it, reminding me of my constant need for God's guiding grace as I make the choices set before me:

O God, Thou knowest that today I must make a decision which is going to affect my whole life. Help me to choose the right way. Grant me Thy guidance, and with it grant me the humble obedience to accept it. Help me not to choose what I want to do, but what Thou dost wish me to do. Grant that I may not be swayed by fear or by hope of gain, by selfish love of ease or comfort or by personal ambition, by the desire to escape or the longing for prestige. Help me today in humble obedience to say to Thee: "Lord, what wilt Thou have me to do?" and then to await Thy guidance, and to accept Thy leading. Hear this my prayer, and send me an answer so clear that I cannot mistake it. This I ask for Thy love's sake. Amen.[25]

Why would a person pray such a prayer when "going for the gusto" is so much more appealing? It sounds pretty preposterous, doesn't it? In fact, such convictions are entirely preposterous when judged by the standards of the world. But those who have encountered the amazing grace of God at the foot of an old rugged cross choose to live this way because the sovereign love of God came down at Christmas and was crucified and resurrected, and because we are utterly convinced that God's saving purposes are being worked out in the realm of history, and nothing will finally stand in the way of their fulfillment.

A New World Is Coming

The sovereignty of God has to do not only with the past and the present but also with the end toward which human history is moving. David Buttrick tells the story of a woman deep in Louisiana, who raised over a dozen children, most of them adopted or foster children. One day, a newspaper reporter asked her why she had done this, and she replied, "I saw a new world a'comin.'"[26] Disciples of Jesus Christ live in a way that seems strange when judged by the expectations of our culture because we see a new world a'comin', and we know there is more to life than meets the eye. The Bible paints the most marvelous portrait of the new world toward which all creation is moving. Paraphrasing a passage in Isaiah, the apostle Paul speaks of the new world a'comin' that "no eye has seen, nor ear heard, nor the human heart conceived, [that] God has prepared for those who love him" (1 Cor. 2:9). And the gospel assures us that, just as the sovereign God created all that is and set the universe in motion, so also will the sovereign God one day resolve all the dissonance of human life into an unrestrained chorus of joy. The book of Revelation offers this vision of the new world that is surely coming by the power of the sovereign Lord:

> Then I saw a new heaven and a new earth; for the first heaven and the first earth had passed away, and the sea was no more. . . . And I heard a loud voice from the throne saying,

> "See, the home of God is among mortals.
> He will dwell with them;
> they will be his peoples,
> and God himself will be with them;
> he will wipe every tear from their eyes.
> Death will be no more;
> mourning and crying and pain will be no more,
> for the first things have passed away."

And the one who was seated on the throne said, "See, I am making all things new." (Rev. 21:1, 3–5a)

No one knows how and when this new world will be fully realized, but we know it has already dawned in Jesus Christ. And because it has dawned in Jesus Christ, nothing can stop it. We are assured of a world where there is no more cancer or chemotherapy, no more broken homes or broken hearts, no more stroke or Alzheimer's disease or crib death or heart disease, no more anger or bitterness or rudeness, no more racism or bigotry of any kind, no more hypocrisy, no more school shootings, no more neglected children, no more substance abuse, no more unwanted babies, no more bellies swollen from hunger, no more pornography, no more rape, no more church fights, no more exploited resources, no more fear, and no more death. It will be a world of boundless joy, as the redeemed community worships the sovereign God in endless doxology, singing:

> "Amen! Blessing and glory and wisdom
> and thanksgiving and honor
> and power and might
> be to our God forever and ever!
> Amen!"
>
> (Rev. 7:12)

Truth 2
God Calls Us
to Be a Holy People

*"You did not choose me but I chose you. And I appointed you to
go and bear fruit."*

(John 15:16a)

The doctrine of election is one of the Christian faith's long-lost doctrines. For both pew and pulpit, it is rarely seen today as anything more than a dusty relic of a day gone by. To begin with, it sounds hopelessly outdated and suggests a hierarchical framework that, in one fell swoop, catapults you into the forbidden zone of political incorrectness. Yet I am convinced that much of what ails the church today is rooted in our collective amnesia concerning this belief that is absolutely central to the faith of the Bible.

The very use of the word "election" brings to mind another theological word that is much misunderstood and maligned today—predestination. It seems almost universally assumed that Presbyterians and predestination fit together like hand and glove, although no one seems to know what predestination means. For some, it means that God predetermined everything I would do during my lifetime. By an inscrutable decree kept hidden until now, God foreordained that I would eat oatmeal for breakfast this morning instead of Cheerios, and that I would wear my blue shirt instead of my green one. But am I really to believe that the Lord of the universe is concerned about the minutiae of my breakfast menu and my choice of shirts? What if I had chosen to begin the day by eating three pounds of chocolate and driving to the church naked? Would God have been the Mover and Shaker behind those ill-fated decisions as well? Such attempts to "theologize" remind me of the well-meaning parishioner who announced to his Sunday school class (and not in an effort to be funny) that he knows God answers prayer because whenever he prays for a good parking place, he usually finds one!

These concerns, however, actually fall under the category of God's *providence* rather than predestination. The doctrine of predestination speaks of the will and intention of God as the driving force behind human destiny. For some Christians, it has meant that, before the foundation of the world, God predestined a select few to the heavenly bliss of everlasting life and, at the same time, foreordained the unlucky masses to fry in the fiery flames of hell for all eternity. This view of predestination (my caricature of it aside) has certainly played a role in the history of the church. According to the Westminster Confession of Faith, "By the decree of God, for the manifestation of his glory, some men and angels are predestinated unto everlasting life, and others foreordained to everlasting death."[1] We also find this understanding of predestination in Calvin, as well as Augustine before him.[2] Not many Presbyterians today find that this view helps them to understand the God of the Bible, yet I still have conversations with folks who come to the Presbyterian Church from other traditions who think this is exactly what we believe. So a word about it is in order.

John Calvin intended the doctrine of predestination to be an immense comfort by affirming that God has taken full responsibility for our salvation. We do not have to spend our lives on the treadmill of legalism. Salvation is not about buying God's favor or proving our self worth by doing good works. Rather, salvation is what *God* does and, from start to finish, it is a matter of God's sovereign and electing grace. For Calvin, this understanding of predestination was the only logical conclusion to which God's sovereignty could lead. If God is truly sovereign, according to Calvin, then some people respond in faith and others do not simply because God wills it.

Presbyterians today have a hard time finding in Calvin's view the comfort he intended. While we believe that God is indeed sovereign, we do not assume that God's sovereignty means that, before the foundation of the world, God damned some people to hell. No doubt, this view of God has loomed large behind the fire and brimstone sermon so flawless at condemnation. Yet I hope we have already laid to rest any notion of God as a capricious Heavenly Tyrant who arbitrarily doles out blessings and curses.

The doctrine of election (or predestination) is indeed a first step in building on the foundation of the sovereignty of God. Because God is truly the all-powerful life force behind the universe, then we have not been left to the devices and desires of our own hearts. In the words of John Leith,

> Predestination means that human life is rooted in the will and the intention of God. . . . Reformed theologians have known that faith, as well as gratitude, love, and self-forgetfulness is a psychologically and historically completely human act, but they have also insisted that faith is first of all the act

of God that elicits the human response. Reformed theologians have always known that psychologically and historically the life of faith and the life of the church were the work of the people of God. Yet, they also insisted that the root of this life was not first in the decision of individuals or of the community but in the election of God.[3]

Election means that, in matters of faith and human destiny, the initiative is always *God's* initiative. Our lives are rooted not in our own purposes, but in *God's*. According to Karl Barth,

> God has . . . the unconditioned priority. It is His act. *His* is and remains the first and decisive Word, *His* is the initiative, *His* is the leadership. How could we see and say it otherwise when we look at Jesus Christ in whom we find man taken up into communion with God?[4]

A relationship with God is never the result of a person's weighing all available options and choosing God, as though choosing God is a reasonable decision among reasonable people. It is a gracious gift from start to finish—undeserved, unearned, and unmerited. " 'Twas grace that taught my heart to fear, and grace my fears relieved. . . ."[5]

Election, in many ways, is a very un-American idea that flies squarely in the face of the way our culture has taught us to think about ourselves. In this "land of the free and home of the brave," we fancy ourselves in complete control of our destinies. Ever since the Pilgrims crossed the Atlantic Ocean to conquer the daunting frontier of a brave New World, we have believed that one's destiny is largely the direct result of pulling yourself up by the bootstraps, rolling up your sleeves, and making your own way in the world because you are, after all, the master of your own destiny. In a certain sense, of course, this is true. No one is going to live my life for me. *I* must make choices, and the choices *I* make will directly affect the quality and character not only of my life but of the lives around me in my small corner of the world. So from one perspective, life is a series of important choices we make on a wide variety of subjects. We choose whom to marry; whether or not to use birth control; whether we'll go to college and, if so, which one; what job we think will provide a sense of lasting fulfillment, or perhaps the coveted pot of gold at the end of the rainbow; whether to live in this house or that; whether to move in one social circle or another. We choose, we choose, and then we choose some more, and somehow, in the midst of our choosing, we come to believe the words of William Ernest Henley:

> I am the master of my fate:
> I am the captain of my soul.[6]

Yet the grace of the cross calls into question our most treasured assumptions about our own power and ability, and from the standpoint of biblical faith, a fallacy of the first order surfaces the moment we think that we are masters of our own destinies (was this not precisely God's bone of contention with Adam and Eve?) and that life somehow begins and ends with our personal choices. When it comes to our relationship with God, hear the words of our Lord: "You did not choose me but *I chose you*, and appointed you to go and bear fruit." And 1 Peter reminds us that disciples of Jesus are not self-appointed: "You are a *chosen* race, a royal priesthood, a holy nation, God's own people. . . ." Whatever else it means that we are God's own people, it begins with the grace of God's choosing.

Yet doesn't becoming a disciple of Jesus Christ require a personal choice? Of course it does. Our Lord also said, "If any want to become my followers, let them deny themselves and take up their cross and follow me" (Mark 8:34), and "Whoever comes to me and does not hate father and mother, wife and children, brothers and sisters, yes, and even life itself, cannot be my disciple" (Luke 14:26). As the Israelites faced the many choices available to them in a pluralistic world, Moses admonished them: "I call heaven and earth to witness against you today that I have set before you life and death, blessings and curses. Choose life so that you and your descendants may live, loving the LORD your God, obeying him, and holding fast to him . . ." (Deut. 30:19–20a). As Israel finally took possession of the promised land, Joshua gathered the twelve tribes together at Shechem and told them in no uncertain terms: "Choose this day whom you will serve, whether the gods your ancestors served in the region beyond the River or the gods of the Amorites in whose land you are living; but as for me and my household, we will serve the LORD" (Josh. 24:15).

Like the twelve tribes entering the land of promise, we too are called to make significant faith choices that grow out of the character and moral fiber of our lives. There are indeed thorny choices to be made by every person who wants to live in the shadow of the cross. I tell our confirmation class each year that the decision to follow Jesus Christ is the most important decision they will ever make, more important than whether or not they play sports, where they will go to college, whom they will eventually choose to marry, or what vocation will end up as their life's work. Confessing Jesus Christ as Lord and Savior is so important, in fact, that we should consider it with the full power of the mind and by searching the very depths of the heart's devotion. Yet our decision to follow Jesus Christ, significant and life-defining as it is, is secondary to *the* decision that God has already made in Jesus Christ to love us and call us to service.

The book of 1 John assures us that "we love because [God] first loved us" (4:19). This affirmation helps us to see divine election as a matter of *being in a relationship of love with God*. John Leith reminds us of Calvin's insistence that God does not deal with us as if we were sticks and stones but as persons.[7] It helps, therefore, to understand election not as a static, impersonal decree of God arbitrarily forced on us, but in terms of a relationship created and sustained by love. People don't fall in love by waking up one morning and saying to themselves, "I think I'll fall in love today." In Leith's words,

> When a person falls in love, there is always something about the person who loves that reaches out and elicits love. Yet the act of love is very much one's own. Perhaps one is never so free and never so truly oneself as in the act of love. Yet every act of love must be explained first of all not in terms of human effort but in terms of a grace that reached out and called it forth.[8]

Election is theological language describing that grace. It announces God's free and sovereign choice to love us in the life, death, and resurrection of Jesus Christ. And the impact of God's love is so enormous, so overwhelming that we freely choose to love God in response.

The best way to understand the electing grace of God, however, is through God's self-revelation in the Bible, so we turn now to two stories of faith from the Old Testament. Both of them come to us from the earliest days of our sacred history, and they reveal not only that God is in charge, but that *God calls us to be a holy people*. But let me offer a word of caution concerning the word "holy." In the Bible, holiness has nothing in the least to do with the holier-than-thou, Goody Two-shoes connotation we often give it today. Rather, in the Bible, to be holy simply means to be set apart by God to serve God—*not* set above, *not* given a superior station in life, but *set apart to serve as a human instrument in the hand of God*. This is the length and breadth and height and depth of God's electing grace. It has nothing to do with being handed a chic life of privilege, but it has everything to do with the good news that "the great fact is God, and the true vocation of every human being is trust in him and loyalty to his cause." As we shall see in the lives of Abraham, Sarah, and Moses, the election of God is an election to service, not privilege, as we endeavor to honor the God who calls us to be a holy people.

Abraham and Sarah, God's Unlikely Choice for a Future

No one knew better than Abraham and Sarah that the story of our faith originates not in ourselves but in the God who calls.[9] Setting out for an unnamed promised land of undisclosed location is not exactly the most sane advice for the person driven by conventional human wisdom. In fact, conventional human wisdom would roundly denounce such a plan and send the person considering it for extensive counseling. Yet the faith of Abraham and Sarah begins with these mind-blowing surprises: 1) life with God is of doubtful promise by human standards; 2) journeying with God is invariably perilous, risky, and loaded with liabilities; and 3) the only way forward is to trust God in a world pocked with uncertainty, building on the foundation "whose architect and builder is God" (Heb. 11:10).

These surprises do not have the appealing ring of popular religion in America, and they definitely are not the message you'll get by tuning in to cable TV's around-the-clock slate of televangelists who want us to believe that a relationship with God is a cozy little matter of financial security and user-friendly religion all around. Voluntarily sign on for a life loaded with liabilities? You've got to be out of your mind! I'll take the user-friendly brand any day, thank you very much! But the Bible reveals a God radically different from the user-friendly gods that litter the landscape of popular religion.

When Abraham and Sarah appear on the scene, the biblical story has reached a critical juncture. Nothing less than the future of God's relationship with the whole of creation is at stake. The human creatures' attempt to build the Tower of Babel (Gen. 11:1–9) comes to an abrupt end, as God frustrates their plan by confusing their language and scattering them abroad over the face of the whole earth. What will God do now? Will God remain faithful to the creation once upon a time pronounced "very good"? Or will God, in total despair, consign the human race to a godforsaken existence?

Enter Abraham and Sarah, who represent God's hope of a new beginning. The hope in their lives, though, is anything but self-evident. Abraham is an old man and Sarah a barren woman. They have managed to miss every opportunity for advancement that came down the pike and have been callously passed over for every promotion. And on top of it all, they have no son. They have consistently failed in the one thing that really matters: no son in a culture where having a son is everything! Does it appear, by even the wildest stretch of the imagination, that they have a future? Indeed not. Yet this future-less couple is called by God literally to pack up their belongings, leave behind kith and kin, and go to an undisclosed land that God will identify only after they make the commitment to go. They will become the father and mother of a great nation that will one day be a blessing to all the families of the earth. Never mind the fact that Sarah has already gone through menopause and long ago forfeited the dream of having a child. What on earth can God be thinking? There isn't anything about Abraham and Sarah that makes them exemplary specimens of the human race, and the promised land isn't a sudden brainstorm that they come up with one morning as a convenient plan to make retirement more interesting. ("Yes, that's what we'll do! We'll spend our golden years parenting a great nation!")

This is why it is so important that we see the story of Abraham and Sarah in terms of God's electing grace. Their human story is, first and foremost, *God's* story, *God's* agenda, *God's* faithfulness graciously given to a categorically wayward creation, *God's* undying hope for the future of the human race. This is not some new God who appears out of nowhere but the same God who created the heavens and the earth and everything that is; the same God who suffered the indignities of rejection by Adam and Eve, the heartbreak of Abel's blood crying out from the earth, and the dismal failure of a so-called new beginning with Noah. And this same God now reaches into the deepest recesses of human hopelessness to create another new beginning. As Walter Brueggemann has written,

> The one who calls the worlds into being now makes a second call. This call is specific. Its object is identifiable in history. The call is addressed to aged Abraham and to barren Sarah. The purpose of the call is to fashion an alternative community in creation gone awry, to embody in human history the power of the blessing. It is the hope of God that in this new family all human history can be brought to the unity and harmony intended by the one who calls.[10]

No, this is not, first of all, the story of Abraham and Sarah and their grand ideas about serving God. Abraham and Sarah aren't at the head of the line for an enterprise called insanity, and neither do they update their résumés in an effort to land a posh spot in what they hope will soon become upwardly mobile careers. *This is something God is doing; it is God's action, God's blessing of a creation still loved, God's sovereign call to a people who will serve as an instrument in reclaiming all the peoples of the earth, God's electing grace in the blinding fog of human rejection.* Abraham and Sarah will be instruments in the hands of Another, flesh and blood vessels of a divine purpose so foreign to their daily, cultural realities that it could only have originated outside of themselves.

This leads us directly to another key theme of the story, namely, that God calls Abraham and Sarah to a radical departure from their current life in order to embrace the new life of which God is personally the architect and maker (cf. Heb. 11:10). In Genesis 12, God speaks directly to Abraham with the unequivocal command:

> "Go from your country and your kindred and your father's house to the land that I will show you. I will make of you a great nation, and I will bless you,

and make your name great, so that you will be a blessing. I will bless those who bless you, and the one who curses you I will curse; and in you all the families of the earth shall be blessed." (Gen. 12:1–3)

The lavish blessing of God is graciously promised, yet the ramifications are unambiguously clear. Abraham—and this is one of the hardest parts for our modern ears—is to "abandon radically all natural roots,"[11] to sever ties with all the cultural realities to which he has grown accustomed. To be faithful to God, he and Sarah must embark on a radical departure and willingly embrace an unthinkable future. In fact, the specific naming of "your country," "your kindred," and "your father's house" spells out the utter particularity of the divine call and the totality of life that God's call encompasses. God surely knows the life-changing pangs of uncertainty that accompany these separations. Gerhard von Rad reminds us that "one must always remember that to leave home and to break ancestral bonds was to expect of ancient [people] almost the impossible."[12] Yet these unlikely servants of God are expected "simply to leave everything behind and entrust [themselves] to God's guidance"[13] with a living faith that "protests against a world that is fixed on what is safe, predictable, and controllable."[14] (Please note that every notion of "volunteerism" in the kingdom of God was, in one fell swoop, just obliterated.)

The truly remarkable thing, of course, is that Abraham and Sarah take God up on the offer of new life—no great soul searching, no weighing all the pros and cons, no playing the devil's advocate just for the sake of argument, no mental gymnastics in an effort to rationalize away the demand at the heart of the promise. Instead, all we get is obedience, plain and simple. The sovereign Lord says, "Go," and Abraham and Sarah get up and go. Later in the story, they both will laugh at this whole scandalous enterprise (which is why their son is named Isaac, which in Hebrew means "laughter"), but at the beginning of the story, they respond with the most remarkable act of solidarity with God's purpose and become models of faith. Together, Abraham and Sarah stand in stark contrast to all the human responses God has received up to this point. Now it will be different as Abraham and Sarah respond with willing surrender, teaching us that faith means embracing the future God promises.[15]

The narrative itself protects us from trivializing Abraham's and Sarah's faith as a piece of pious pie in the sky. As Walter Brueggemann reminds us, their moments of faith are profound, but their faith does not occur in a vacuum. Their feet, just like ours, are made of clay. Not only do they laugh at the promise of a son in their ripe old age, but they are also portraits of our own doubts and fears as they question whether or not God can be trusted. Abraham enters into deception to save his skin (Gen. 12:10–20, 20:1–18); he takes

Hagar as an alternative wife, just in case God isn't a keeper of promises (16:1–16); and he clings to Hagar's son, Ishmael, the product of his own scheming, when God's purpose is still a son born of Sarah (17:15–22).[16] The story reveals a man and woman who are the same vulnerable, flesh-and-blood creatures we all are. Yet in the midst of their deepest doubts and darkest fears, they give of themselves what God has wanted from the very beginning— *trust.* And they embrace the future God promises.

Embracing God's future, however, means living as God's chosen people, and this brings us to what, for many people, is the most objectionable, even offensive, part of the doctrine of election. The phrase itself, *God's chosen people,* seems out of step with egalitarian concerns for mutuality and equality. After all, doesn't Israel's or the church's "chosenness" suggest an exclusivity whereby a privileged few are "in" but all the unlucky, miserable wretches of the earth are "out"? And isn't it a potential source of the most outrageous arrogance? This is precisely what it would mean in any story except this story, and with any god except the God of the Bible.

When God approaches Abraham and Sarah with the implausible possibility that they will surrender their lives, God's purpose is to bless all the families of the earth. The net result of their election is not the exclusion of all the other poor slobs on the face of the earth. God "chose Israel not *instead of* but *for the sake of* all others, to be 'a light to the nations' so that the justice of God might reach to the ends of the earth" (italics added).[17] Abraham's and Sarah's "chosenness" has nothing whatever to do with being charter members of an elite country club for senior citizens and, as we see in the rest of the story, they end up anywhere and everywhere but on Easy Street. The purpose of God is to reclaim the *whole* of creation. A son will be born to this one man and woman and, through the promised son, their progeny will become the nation of Israel, which will be God's instrument in bringing all the nations of the earth back into a faithful relationship with the sovereign Lord of all history. "The call to Sarah and Abraham has to do not simply with the forming of Israel but with the re-forming of creation, the transforming of the nations."[18] It will be a long and circuitous journey punctuated by many false starts and wrong turns. The rocky path will bring the people of God to many crossroads where decisions will not be easy. Yet in and through it all, the faithfulness of God will endure, and Paul will write centuries later,

> Just as Abraham "believed God, and it was reckoned to him as righteousness," so, you see, those who believe are the descendants of Abraham. And the scripture, foreseeing that God would justify the Gentiles by faith, declared the gospel beforehand to Abraham, saying, "All the Gentiles shall be blessed in you." (Gal. 3:6–8)

The election of God, therefore, is election to service, not privilege. In the first instance, election is a source of incomparable joy, but it is joy that finds its deepest satisfaction and most enduring fulfillment in doing the will of God. In declaring the gospel beforehand, the Old Testament teaches us what we will one day learn from our Savior. In Matthew 20:17–28, the mother of James and John comes to Jesus with her two sons in tow. They have just been discussing how delicious it is to be on the inside track with the Messiah. In fact, such connections in the kingdom of God far exceed their wildest dreams. Their mother, however, has high ambitions for her sons, and she suddenly envisions cashing in on the perks of this unexpectedly gratuitous relationship. She isn't content that James and John have been given cabinet posts; she wants them to be Jesus' closest and most trusted advisors. So she asks Jesus to promise that, when the kingdom comes, both of her sons will be given senior positions, one sitting at his right hand and the other at his left. After all, she has always wanted only the best for her sons, and like every conscientious mother, she is only thinking of their future. But Jesus will have no part of the greedy, grasping ways of this well-meaning mother and the two sons who no doubt put her up to it. "You evidently haven't heard a thing I've said," he replies. "Whoever wishes to be great among you must be your servant, and whoever wishes to be first among you must be your slave; just as the Son of Man came not to be served but to serve, and to give his life a ransom for many."

Moses, an Unlikely Candidate for the Ministry

Then there is the case of an obscure man named Moses in whom we also see the sovereign power of God to grasp a person's life and not let go.[19] As the curtain rises, hundreds of years have passed since that fateful day when Abraham and Sarah packed their bags and began the most outlandish of all journeys toward the rich land of God's promise. The promise, however, has not yet materialized, and the Hebrew people have been slaves of the Egyptian pharaoh for 430 years.

> He [Pharaoh] said to his people, "Look, the Israelite people are more numerous and more powerful than we. Come, let us deal shrewdly with them, or they will increase and, in the event of war, join our enemies and fight against us and escape from the land." Therefore they set taskmasters over them to oppress them with forced labor. . . . The Egyptians became ruthless in imposing tasks on the Israelites, and made their lives bitter with hard service in mortar and brick and in every kind of field labor. (Exod. 1:9–11a, 13–14a)

Enter Moses. Aside from the fact that he is quietly tending the flock of his father-in-law, Jethro, the main thing we know about Moses is this: In a fit of rage, he killed an Egyptian for mistreating one of the slaves and was forced to flee for his life. There he is in Exodus 3, doing what any fugitive from justice would do—hunkering down to mind his own business and hoping beyond hope that Pharaoh's gestapo won't hunt him down. But while he may be resourceful enough to escape Pharaoh's attention, there isn't a profile low enough to escape the searching eye of God. Out of the blue, God appears on the scene uninvited. Speaking from the midst of a bush that is on fire but not being consumed, God announces that Moses has been chosen to lead the Hebrew slaves to freedom. God has seen the affliction of the slaves and has heard their cries of anguish rising up from the shackles of oppression. In tender love and compassion, God is going to free the slaves and, wonder of wonders, Moses, the hunkered-down, hot-headed fugitive, is the chosen servant of their redemption. The problem, though, is that Moses is not the least bit interested.

"Any chance you'll reconsider?" Moses asks God.

"Not on your life" is God's stubborn answer.

"What if I told you I'm really not cut out for the job? That I'm not the most respected person around, and that the idea of speaking in public gives me the shivers?"

"It really wouldn't matter, because I know you better than you know yourself, and you're the one for the job. I've already made up my mind, and there's no turning back."

"Then let me be totally honest here: *Read my lips; I don't want the job!*

"Let *me* be totally honest here: *You, Moses, are the one I have chosen, so you can forget all your lame excuses. You can like it or lump it, but you're in for the long haul!*"

Again, please note that the popular notion of "volunteerism" rampant in today's church (as though discipleship to the Crucified One can somehow be understood as "volunteers for Jesus") just suffered an untimely demise. And I can't help but think of Moses and his excuses every year as our officer nominating committee begins working on a slate of new elders and deacons. Moses wasn't sitting around just waiting to be invited to the great honor of serving God by taking on the most hair-raising implausibility imaginable. Neither does the call of Moses paint a portrait of an eager beaver sitting on the front row, expectantly waving his arm and pleading, "Let me! Let me! I'll do it! I'll do it!" In fact, Moses offers every conceivable excuse, but to no avail. The sovereign God will not be deterred. Like Abraham and Sarah before him, Moses comes face to face with the inescapable reality that "the great fact is God," and now "trust in him and loyalty to his cause" will be the foundation on which the rest of his life will be built. Once more, we see that faith is embracing the unsettling new future that God promises, reaching out in the darkness of uncertainty to take hold of the One who has already laid hold of us.

The call of Moses returns, as well, to some of the other main themes of election already experienced by Abraham and Sarah, first of all bearing witness to the fact that the story of redemption is unequivocally *God's* story. Moses was not a person who presumably had the good sense to follow his best instincts and thereby find God. In fact, when God first appeared, Moses didn't even know God's name! Instead, it was just the opposite; God found Moses.

The job to which Moses is called will end up eating his lunch more times than he can count. The journey will be long and arduous, and the landscape littered with the worship of false gods. The freed band of Hebrew slaves will endlessly wander in the wilderness surrounding Mount Sinai before any sign or semblance of the promised land appears. Their hearts will be ripe for the despair that is born of their deepest and darkest doubts. As they cross the threshold of an uncharted and, in many ways, unwanted frontier, they will conclude that God didn't really mean the promise in the first place, that Moses is certifiably nuts, and that they all must have been lunatics for ever leaving behind the mouth-watering leeks, cucumbers, and melons they had regularly enjoyed in Egypt. They may have been measly, mistreated, contemptuous slaves, but at least they ate three squares a day, unlike conditions in this god-forsaken wasteland. But the faithfulness of God will once again hold them up in every dark night of the soul and give them the hope of a new tomorrow even when there are doubts aplenty that tomorrow will ever come.

Jesus Christ and God's Electing Grace

The call of Abraham and Sarah, and the call of Moses, are not isolated illustrations of the electing grace of God. The fact that their vulnerable lives of clay are so totally and irrevocably commandeered into service by the sovereign Lord of the universe is emblematic of the claim of God throughout the Bible, and this brings us to the heart and soul of election: *We see God's electing grace most clearly in the love of Jesus Christ.* The Second Helvetic Confession says this of our election: "Let Christ, therefore be the looking glass, in whom we may contemplate our predestination [election]."[20] Jesus Christ, says Calvin, is the "clearest mirror of free election."[21] Indeed, he is the mirror in which we encounter God's love for all creation. Jesus Christ is the elect One who reveals the truth that God is for us, not against us, and that God has a plan "to gather up all things in him" (Eph. 1:10). All the promises of God find their "Yes" in Jesus Christ (2 Cor. 1:20). The promise to Abraham of a land flowing with milk and honey ultimately finds its fulfillment in Jesus of Nazareth, as does the promise to Moses of a community redeemed and free. The election of a people who will one day be a blessing to all the families of the earth finds its "Yes" in Jesus Christ. And the assurance that death cannot hold us captive finds its "Amen" in the Good Shepherd who lays down his life for his sheep.

Notice how Paul begins his letter to the Ephesians by speaking of election and redemption in the same breath. Affirming that God "chose us in Christ before the foundation of the world," Paul writes, "He destined us for adoption as his children through Jesus Christ. . . . In him we have redemption through his blood, the forgiveness of our trespasses, according to the riches of his grace that he lavished on us" (1:4–8a). We are assured of our destiny as God's children because of the cross of Jesus Christ. There is an irrevocable link between being chosen in Christ before the foundation of the world and being redeemed through the blood of Christ. God's electing grace and our redemption in Christ are finally inseparable.

This is the pure joy of the gospel. As we look into the face of Jesus Christ on the cross, "the clearest mirror of free election," we see that God has personally taken on all the broken promises and violated trust and shattered hopes and raped innocence and petty jealousies and crumbled dreams and fearful tomorrows that try to define us. And God promises that none of these will have the last word over us. Therefore, asks Paul, "Who will bring any charge against God's elect?" and "Who will separate us from the love of Christ?"

> Will hardship, or distress, or persecution, or famine, or nakedness, or peril, or sword? . . . No, in all of these things we are more than conquerors through him who loved us. For I am convinced that neither death, nor life, nor angels, nor rulers, nor things present, nor things to come, nor powers, nor height, nor depth, nor anything else in all creation will be able to separate us from the love of God in Christ Jesus our Lord. (Rom. 8:33ff.)

No wonder Jesus could say, "Be of good cheer, I have overcome the world!" (John 16:33b, RSV).

What Does Election Have to Do with My Life?

I hope it is apparent by now that election is not a purely academic subject that belongs in a textbook for seminarians, but that it is one way of describing

God's gracious descent into the very fiber of human life. It comforts and assures us of God's eternal love, which can never be taken away from us. But you still may be wondering, "What on earth does this have to do with how I live my life in one small corner of the world?" First of all, the electing grace of God gives us a radically new starting point. No longer is my personal plight the exclusive vantage point from which I view my life and the world around me. My starting point is no longer my cultural identity or my genetic makeup or my racial-ethnic heritage or my political persuasion or my sexuality or my socioeconomic status or my flawed history. It is quite true that each of these aspects of my identity significantly shapes my life experiences, my view of the world around me, and my theological temperament. But none of them is the beginning and end of my person. Through the electing grace of God, *Jesus Christ* is the beginning and end of my person, which means that my election as a child of God carries with it a divine summons to bring all of my cultural identity and genetic makeup and racial-ethnic heritage and political persuasion and sexuality and socioeconomic status and flawed history under the sovereign lordship of Jesus Christ. As strange as this sounds to modern people who strive to have all the parts of their personhood publicly affirmed by the church and society, the elect community knows better and does otherwise. Like Abraham and Sarah, we, too, are called to "abandon radically all natural roots," thereby severing ties with cultural realities we have come to cherish. As thorny and even offensive as this sounds, such is the nature of the divine call and the totality of life that the electing grace of God encompasses. Like Moses, we will experience God's deaf ear to our lame and self-centered excuses and finally come to terms with the God who, in saving us from our self-destructive ways, sends us forth across the strangest and most perilous of all frontiers. Make no mistake, the electing grace of God announces that, first and foremost, we have to do with the Lord who says, *You are mine!*

This, of course, is not the way today's church does business, and this is one of the primary reasons that the church is torn apart by an endless array of special-interest groups that help to send us racing toward schism. The only answer I know is this: God calls us to repent by turning anew to Jesus Christ, the mirror of our election, and by acknowledging *him alone* as the starting point of our lives. In a chapter about the cultural captivity of Western Christianity, Lesslie Newbigin has written,

> The gospel is not a set of beliefs that arise or could arise from empirical observation of the whole human experience. It cannot be based on inductive reasoning. It is the announcement of a name and a fact that offer the starting point for the whole lifelong experience of understanding and coping with experience. It is a new starting point. To accept it means a new

beginning, a radical conversion. We cannot side-step that necessity. It has always been the case that to believe means to turn around and face in a different direction, to be a dissident, to swim against the stream.[22]

I can hear that familiar voice in the congregation: "Now you've quit preachin' and gone to meddlin'!" Precisely. The electing grace of God *meddles* in our lives. It challenges even our most cherished cultural assumptions and calls us to become a community of dissidents, swimming against the stream.

The Wideness of God's Electing Grace

As we become a community of dissidents, we do well to remember that the doctrine of election leaves an indelibly positive mark on the way we think of God, the way we understand ourselves as servants of God, and the way we regard others. All too often, the discussion of election ends up in a speculative game of "who's in and who's out?"—a kind of Wheel-of-Fortune for Christians. From my Sunday school experience as a youth to my years as a pastor, I couldn't begin to count the number of times I have heard a Sunday school class become embroiled in a steamy debate over the insider-outsider rub of this doctrine. And, in my experience, the discussion inevitably ends up being purely speculative, inappropriately condemning, and entirely a waste of time. I have never seen it fail; a member of the class will use election to denounce, in sonorous tones, all the unbelievers of the world. And, of course, that person usually presumes to have an inside track on exactly whom God is saving and whom God has decided to fry in unmerciful hell. If this kind of discussion occurs, from time to time, in the friendly Presbyterian church on the corner, you can be sure that it occurs in spades in all the most popular forms of religion today. Tune in to one of the televangelists on cable TV and see if judgment and condemnation are not part and parcel of popular religion in America.

This is not, however, the way that Reformed Christians read the Bible or understand the Christian faith. The only posture for the person who is part of the elect community of faith is the posture of *gratitude and humility*, pure and simple. Inclusion in the household of faith should never be used as a self-righteous hammer of condemnation—*never*. And it should never lead to puffed-up arrogance. The electing grace of God corrects every attempt to reduce the people of God's world for whom Jesus Christ died into categories that make us feel smugly superior to others. The emphasis of election, from beginning to end, is positive and hopeful, full of promise and overflowing with grace. It is intended to build up, not tear down. In the words of Karl Barth,

The elect [person] is chosen in order that the circle of election—that is, the circle of those who recognise and confess Jesus Christ in the world—should not remain stationary or fixed, but open up and enlarge itself, and therefore grow and expand and extend. . . . He will not weary in his service towards [others], nor will he ever be disloyal to it, because of any self-made judgments of his own concerning them. It belongs to God Himself to determine and to know what it means that God was reconciling the world unto himself (2 Cor. 5[19]). The concern of the elect is always the 'ministry of reconciliation' (2 Cor. 5[18]), and no other.[23]

For this reason, the Second Helvetic Confession says, "We are to have a good hope for all."[24]

What would the church be like today if the persons in every pew and pulpit understood themselves to be elect children of the sovereign Lord of the universe who have been commandeered into service? How might the worship and work of the church become redefined if we were willingly and gladly and thankfully to accept our commission from Christ to reach out in his name to all creation? This is the meaning of election. On any given day, it may sound utterly crazy to us, but God's purpose in Christ is a far-flung purpose of love *for all people*, and the electing grace of God sends us out in the world to work toward that day when, as Paul says, all things will be united in Christ, things in heaven and things on earth (Eph. 1:10). What a glorious, wonderful, joyous commission!

Truth 3
Jesus Christ Reveals God's Love

But God proves his love for us in that while we still were sinners Christ died for us.

(Rom. 5:8)

In a sermon, John Claypool relates the story of a small child who had recently learned to write. Sitting in worship one Sunday morning, she wrote these words and handed them to her parents: "Dear Mom and Dad, I love you. Do you love me? Please answer by circling the Yes or the No."[1] This is the question that haunts all of our lives. Dear God, do you love me? I need to know. I need to know *now* in the hurt I feel today, in my disappointment with the fool I've been, in my callous ways with others, in my failure to forgive as I have been forgiven. I need to know, Lord, that your love is stronger than my sin, that despite the things I've said and done, you love me still.

One of the most insatiable hungers of the human heart is to know that "God is love" (1 John 4:8, 16) and to know it not just in three little words printed in the text of the Bible but deep down in the engulfing shadows of our personal guilt. Just now, though, we have come to a particularly prickly point in our journey to the good news of Jesus Christ, namely, our willingness to face head-on issues of personal culpability as we confront the sin at the root of our guilt. My experience as a pastor has taught me that modern Christians, even Presbyterians who traditionally have faced up to sin with brutal honesty, tend to grow edgy when the subject of sin crops up. If the truth be told, most of us are rather like St. Augustine, whose prayer was, "O Lord, give me continence and chastity, but not yet,"[2] or perhaps like the young boy who was overheard to say in his nightly prayers, "Dear God, if you can't make me a better boy, don't worry about it! I'm having a real good time like I am!"

There are numerous reasons for our difficulty in being honest about our sinfulness. For one thing, prevailing attitudes both in the pew and the pulpit have substantial cultural underpinnings that spawn all manner of lies about who we really are in the presence of God. The "anything goes" mantra is part and parcel of our culture of tolerance and inclusiveness, both of which have become sacrosanct in today's church. If you speak too explicitly of sin, then someone is likely to feel judged or excluded. And even worse, you might be perceived as intolerant, which is itself insufferably intolerable, not to mention the sworn enemy of a flourishing pluralism. All lifestyles, this line of reasoning goes, are equally good, so long as those involved are sincere and no one gets hurt. And all beliefs are equally valid because they are simply different shades of the truth. So how are we to deal honestly with the destructive realities of sin in a church that has been domesticated by its surrounding culture?

The devil-made-me-do-it approach to sin also runs rampant in the church today. This is the stance that Adam and Eve adopted when God confronted them with their sin, and it never ceases to be an enticing alternative to facing one's personal culpability. You don't like the way I am? Then get over it, because I'm not to blame. My genes make me behave this way, or the way my parents raised me, or the culture I grew up in, or the lack of love I was given as a teenager, or the sibling rivalry that never got resolved, or the fact that nobody ever really gave me a chance in life. One would expect a secular culture to exchange the truth about God for a lie (Rom. 1:25), but the frightening thing is that even the church finds satisfaction in parroting these lies learned from the prevailing culture.

A few illustrations from life in the church will help. One day, the mother of two young daughters (making no attempt to conceal her not inconsiderable irritation) said to her Sunday school class, "I just hate the part of the worship service where we have the confession of sin. It's not healthy for our children to get such a negative view of themselves, and at church, of all places. It might damage their self esteem." Someone else quickly spoke up in wholehearted agreement, "The Christian faith is supposed to be positive, and I resent having my nose rubbed in the dirt of sin week after week. After all, I'm not even guilty of most of the sins printed in the prayer of confession, so why should I pray it? It doesn't even apply to me."

Or consider the case of a friend of mine in seminary who often timed his entrance into chapel services so that he would arrive after the confession of sin. He simply didn't believe he was all that bad. He tried to follow Jesus Christ, he worked intentionally at being a sensitive and caring person, and he endeavored to make responsible choices and live peaceably with others. "So why should I go to chapel and confess sins that I don't feel I'm guilty of?" he asked.

Then there is the case of the Reluctant Presbyterian that was shared with me by a pastor who was teaching a class on Presbyterian beliefs. Some of the folks in her church had said they wanted to get back to the basics, and she took them at their word. She announced the class with a sense of personal excitement and soon found that her enthusiasm was contagious. As the course progressed, however, the contagion evaporated as some of her congregants became visibly upset over some of our core Presbyterian beliefs. But it was the discussion of sin that drove some of them to the very edge of civility. One Sunday morning, she called the class's attention to one of the great hymns of the church, which says, in part,

> Ah, holy Jesus, how hast Thou offended,
> That man to judge Thee hath in hate pretended . . . ?
> Who was the guilty? Who brought this upon Thee?
> Alas, my treason, Jesus, hath undone Thee!
> 'Twas I, Lord Jesus, I it was denied Thee:
> I crucified Thee.[3]

An agitated discussion then ensued over the suggestion that we ourselves, by our words and actions and motives, have actually hated God, and that *our* treason nailed and continues to nail Jesus to the cross. Some members of the class were aghast that respectable Presbyterians who strive to live decent lives should believe such negative things about themselves and others. One member argued adamantly, "I don't go out of my way to stab anyone in the back, and I try to live by the Golden Rule, so I refuse to say that I hate God. In fact, I'm on God's side, not against him." He went on to agree that there are, of course, deplorable sinners in the world—murderers and rapists and the like— but he resolutely refused to admit any treason in the fertile soil of his respectable life. He, after all, occupied an enviable position in the business community and was part of the affluent white-collar crowd known as the movers and shakers who knew how to get things done. And to top it off, he was an exemplary family man, who lived in a lovely home replete with a devoted wife and picture-perfect children who were being handed the world on a silver platter. Perhaps it was people like him whom T. S. Eliot had in mind when he wrote,

> Half the harm that is done in this world
> Is due to people who want to feel important.
> They don't mean to do harm—but the harm does not interest them.
> Or they do not see it, or they justify it
> Because they are absorbed in the endless struggle
> To think well of themselves.[4]

Or, better yet, maybe the case of the Reluctant Presbyterian illustrates to perfection this claim of Calvin:

> Nothing pleases man more than the sort of alluring talk that tickles the pride that itches in his very marrow. Therefore, in nearly every age, when anyone publicly extolled human nature in most favorable terms, he was listened to with applause. But however great such commendation of human excellence is that teaches man to be satisfied with himself, it does nothing but delight in its own sweetness; indeed, it so deceives as to drive those who assent to it into utter ruin.[5]

Calvin, no doubt, would have agreed with the pastor who has observed, "We have so emphasized a positive self-image that there are some people today who can strut sitting down."[6]

With such obstacles in view, we are reminded that the very lifeblood of the gospel is a gracious and loving balm "to heal the sinsick soul."[7] Without the sinsick soul, Jesus Christ is not needed. Without the sinsick soul, the church is merely a group of like-minded people who do amazingly well with their lives and are there to applaud one another on their successes and achievements. Our Lord, however, espoused a radically different view of the community of faith when he said that "those who are well have no need of a physician, but those who are sick; I have come to call not the righteous but sinners to repentance" (Luke 5:31–32).[8] At its core, the church is a hospital for sinners. Tragically, though, the church has sometimes failed to proclaim this vital center of the church's life. The God of the Bible has sometimes been depicted as a wrath-mongering deity whose main purpose is condemning not just sin but also (and maybe even especially) the sinner. When I was growing up, this view often gelled in a mental picture of God as the original grumpy old man who was constantly on the war path and, even in the best of moments, in a more rancorous mood than any man, woman, or child could possibly endure. But the Bible is not the story of a permanently ill-tempered curmudgeon poised to whack anybody and everybody the moment they step out of line, and God is mocked when the gospel is reduced to such "empty deceit" (Col. 2:8). The gospel of the Son of God hanging on a tree for the salvation of the world—*that* is the central reality that God has given us life and breath and undying gratitude to proclaim. To recall the words of the old gospel hymn, "I am Thine, O Lord, I have heard Thy voice, and it told *Thy love* to me. . . ."[9]

It, therefore, is crucial that we understand the essentially redemptive nature of the gospel. In fact, it is only because of God's sacrificial love in Jesus Christ that we are able even to recognize the ruinous ways of sin in our lives. As Gary

A. Anderson helpfully observes in commenting on his reading of Karl Barth, human beings never come to understand their fallen condition simply by contemplating their sinful actions.

> The fathomless depth of sin can only be glimpsed under the tutelage of the Redeemer. . . . The notion of human sin and fallenness is nothing other than a considered reflection on the unmerited and unfathomable moment of salvation.[10]

To be sure, many passages in the Bible speak of divine judgment and wrath, but in the broad scope of the Bible's message, the judgment and wrath of God are never ends in themselves; they always serve the cleansing, renewing purpose of God's redemptive love. The judgment of God in the Bible is steadfastly larger than divine punishment, and the wrath of God exists not for the destruction of but *for the sake of* God's beloved. Just as we encounter God's electing grace supremely in Jesus Christ, so also do we find God's judgment. For Jesus Christ is "the very dying form of One who suffered there for me."[11] It is he who has been judged in our place. And, because of this, the gospel gives us the assurance for which we all hunger and thirst: *Friends, believe the good news of the gospel. In Jesus Christ, we are forgiven. Thanks be to God!*

We, therefore, face up to "our sinful nature prone to evil and slothful in good,"[12] (as the traditional prayer of confession puts it) as those who stand before the throne of grace. We learn the jagged realities of our alienation from God and each other peculiarly through the lens of redemption by which we are mercifully delivered from the jaws of death, freed from the yawning chasm of self-destruction, and set firmly on the church's one foundation, Jesus Christ our Lord.

With this clearly in mind, we turn to two biblical passages, both of which depict our human predicament in graphic terms. Surely it is on the basis of such moments in our sacred history that Paul would later write that "all have sinned and fall short of the glory of God" (Rom. 3:23). First, we return to Adam and Eve. What do the first days of their disobedience teach us about ourselves?

Adam and Eve

In God's good creation, Adam and Eve enjoyed full, abundant communion both with God and each other.[13] It was a scene of inconceivable delight, magnificent beyond our wildest imaginings, running over with life, teeming with promise. It was not a world, however, void of boundaries. In giving Adam and Eve every blessing of the garden of Eden, God was unequivocally clear about one prohibition: "You may freely eat of every tree of the garden; but of the tree of the knowledge of good and evil you shall not eat, for in the day that you eat of it you shall die" (Gen. 2:16–17).

The rest, as they say, is history. The serpent tempted Eve with the delicious possibility of equality with God: "You won't die, Eve, if you eat some of this astonishing fruit. Just look at it—how mouth-watering, how luscious, how divine! Trust me on this; it's the tastiest fruit in the garden, and the only reason God doesn't want you to have it is that it will make you like God, knowing good and evil. Isn't that what you really want deep down inside—to be like God? Never mind what God said. It's time to grow up now and make your own decisions." So Adam and Eve willingly and intentionally crossed the one boundary God had given them because they wanted to be their own god, accountable only to themselves. They enjoyed a delectable meal of forbidden fruit, and immediately the gathering clouds of doom threatened them with a fury they could not have imagined. Suddenly aware, for the first time, of their nakedness, they made loincloths for themselves out of fig leaves, for they could no longer delight in each other's nakedness without a sense of embarrassment and shame. Paradise was already lost, and the good creation of God soiled by human disobedience.

When they heard the sound of the Lord God walking in the garden, Adam and Eve swiftly hid themselves. They were guilty and they knew it, and now their guilt had erected an unscalable barrier between them and the very God who created and loved them beyond all measure. The Lord called out to Adam, "Where are you?"

Adam answered, "I heard the sound of you in the garden, and I was afraid, because I was naked, so I hid myself."

"Who told you that you were naked?" God asked. "Have you crossed the one boundary I gave you? Have you eaten the forbidden fruit?"

"It was the woman whom you gave to be with me! It's not my fault! If you're looking for someone to blame, blame her!"

"Oh, no, you don't!" argued Eve. "The serpent tricked me, and I ate. If you really want to know how the whole thing went down, *the devil made me do it!*"

But the Lord God will tolerate no excuses, no finger-pointing, no sordid attempts to deflect the blame of which all are guilty. Personal culpability is now center stage, as God refuses to let them lay the blame at anyone's feet but their own, and Adam and Eve are sentenced to the heartbreaking wounds and incessant vulnerability of life east of Eden.

As I suggested earlier, the story of Adam and Eve is *our* story, the tale of *our* disobedience. It is impossible to read this story in the context of the whole

Bible without coming to a term that we moderns sometimes find unsettling, if not downright unacceptable: *original sin*. Now I realize that the mere mention of original sin is enough to make some of you want to close this book right here and now, never to reopen it. At best, it sounds like it belongs in a dictionary of archaic terms, an antiquated relic of a bygone era and hopelessly out of step with the sophisticated airs of the twenty-first century. At worst, it suggests the most unflattering definition of ourselves conceivable, the sort of definition, in fact, that requires a good antidepressant and several years of psychotherapy to overcome. As Edward T. Oaks has accurately observed,

> No doctrine inside the precincts of the Christian Church is received with greater reserve and hesitation, even to the point of outright denial, than the doctrine of original sin. . . . [E]ven in those denominations that pride themselves on their adherence to the orthodox dogmas of the once-universal Church, the doctrine of original sin is met with either embarrassed silence, outright denial, or at a minimum a kind of halfhearted lip service that does not exactly deny the doctrine but has no idea how to place it inside the devout life.[14]

But before we dismiss it out of hand, let's look more closely not at what we think it *might* mean, but at what it *does* mean. For the doctrine of original sin grows directly out of the Bible and is one of the essentials of Reformed thought.

First of all, original sin does not mean, as some have wrongly supposed, that sin is inherited biologically through the natural process of an egg and sperm doing their thing. Neither does it mean that, because sex is evil (an unbiblical notion in and of itself), sin has been passed on to every generation since Adam and Eve through the act of sexual intercourse (no, sin is not a sexually transmitted disease).

Rather, original sin means that Adam and Eve are a reflection of our own self-interest and self-absorption, our own transgression of God-given boundaries, our own propensity for exchanging the truth about God for a lie (Rom. 1:25). Peering into the mirror of Adam and Eve, we glimpse the treason of our own ravenous hunger for autonomy and the wasteful squandering of the good gifts of God. In other words, what Adam and Eve did, we all do. Their sin is our sin, and we see ourselves in their act of overreaching their God-given destiny. Original sin means simply that being a sinner is inescapable. No person is ever born into the world so totally pure and spotless that a sinless life is an option. This is why King David (to whom we shall turn momentarily) prays with such brutal honesty, "Indeed, I was born guilty, a sinner when my mother conceived me" (Ps. 51:5). In other words, no one can choose *not* to be a sinner.[15]

Better than any explanation of sin, however, is a picture of sin, so we turn now to another Bible picture that brings the predicament of sin into sharp relief. As you read this story, bear in mind that the protagonist is not some lowlife villain (at least on the surface) but a fine, upstanding, respectable specimen of the human race. The protagonist is none other than God's chosen servant, King David.

David and Bathsheba

In 2 Samuel 11 and 12, we find the remarkable story of King David, Bathsheba, Uriah the Hittite, and a prophet of God named Nathan.[16] As the curtain rises, it's the time of year "when kings go out to battle," but this year David stays at home in Jerusalem, sending Joab to act as commander-in-chief in his place. One day, after a little afternoon siesta, as David is walking around on the roof of his house, he casts his eye with pride over the great city he has conquered. He remembers the battle that secured the prize of Jerusalem and the sense of accomplishment that swelled within him as he transformed it into his capital city. And he recalls, no doubt, the many springs when he himself had gone forth to battle and the many victories he had won, each making his power as the monarch of Israel more secure. Now in the gentle breeze of late afternoon, as David ponders his great prowess as a warrior and king, his eye falls on a lovely woman taking a bath across the way. He, of course, has seen her before, each time reveling in her ravishing beauty. But somehow her nakedness is lovelier than David had imagined, and he can't keep his eyes off of her fair skin . . . her voluptuous breasts . . . her sensuous flesh. By now, David is aflame with the fires of lust, and his mind races to touch her, to have her, to conquer her. (I hope this lays to rest any notion that the Bible is out of touch with the real lives of real people!)

As with so many cases where lust is the lead player, the problem is that the woman, Bathsheba by name, is a married woman. Her husband, in fact, is Uriah the Hittite, who just happens to be out risking life and limb at the moment, fighting David's war. This is only a minor complication, however, for a person of David's prowess. If he can conquer a city and win a war, surely he can figure a way to conquer a married woman. So David sends for Bathsheba, she comes to him, and the king of Israel enjoys a sleazy afternoon romp in the hay with good old Uriah's wife. But again, as is usually the case in such situations, the king's troubles have only just begun. As a result of David's afternoon delight, Bathsheba becomes pregnant.

What to do? A sleazy scheme, of course, will make an apt companion to the sleazy affair. David sends for Uriah to come home on furlough, thinking that surely he will sleep with his wife and everyone will think the baby is Uriah's. But Uriah is unwilling to have intercourse with Bathsheba because it would be dishonorable for him to spill his seed in the conjugal pleasures of his wife's bed while his comrades are spilling their blood on the king's battlefield. So the plot thickens. The king wines and dines Uriah, thinking that, after the third or fourth drink, surely to goodness, Uriah's overactive hormones will cause him to lose his scruples in the heat of passion and enjoy an evening in bed with his wife. But even that doesn't work, for Uriah is a man of integrity and his sense of honor will not be breached.

Now David's unflinching determination to save his rear drives him to an even darker deed. Via a written order to Joab delivered by Uriah's own hand, David engineers Uriah's death on the battlefield. Finally! The deceitful scheme has worked! With Uriah conveniently out of the way, David takes Bathsheba for his own wife, thinking that he has safely tidied up both his adulterous affair and his culpability in the murder of his next-door neighbor. But now the plot thickens even more.

David soon discovers that his core problem goes beyond a mere fling between the sheets, and even beyond his cold-blooded conspiracy to have Uriah the Hittite murdered. David's core problem, you see, is *God*, and David is on the brink of learning that God will have none of our take-what-you-can-get-and-sweep-your-trash-under-the-rug approach to life. The anger of the Lord burns hot, and Nathan the prophet is called on to provide David with a very distinctive brand of pastoral care. He begins by telling David a story. There were two men, one rich and one poor. The rich man had an abundance of flocks, but the poor man was destitute, except for one little ewe lamb. One day, the rich man was entertaining a visitor and needed a lamb to cook for dinner. Since he couldn't bring himself to sacrifice one of his own lambs, he went out and stole his neighbor's one ewe lamb and then proceeded to kill it, cook it, and serve it on a silver platter. At this, David's anger is kindled, and he says to Nathan, "As the Lord lives, the man who has done this deserves to die. . . ." Nathan says to David, "You are the man!" Then after Nathan gives David an unflinching piece of God's mind on the subjects of adultery, stealing, and murder, David falls to his knees in penitence. "I have sinned against the Lord," he confesses. And Nathan says to David, "Now the Lord has put away your sin; you shall not die."

This is one of the most remarkable moments in our sacred history. David has just committed some of the most abhorrent sins imaginable. He has used his God-given power as king to violate Bathsheba, to murder Uriah, and to make innocent Joab the instrument of his sleazy deed. He has acquiesced to his basest desires, and treated the human beings around him as mere objects of those desires. And what does David get? Forgiveness. *God's forgiveness*, of all things! Outrageous, isn't it? To be sure, David will bear the heavy consequences of his actions. The child conceived in his illicit affair with Bathsheba will die, and David's life will never be the same because of what he has done. But in spite of it all, David is forgiven.

As we face the ravages of our own sin, David's attitude should help to shape our own. It is instructive, for example, that not once does David argue with Nathan. He doesn't get defiant or defensive, and neither does he try to put a pretty face on the ugliness he has done. He doesn't attempt to blame it on the power of lust that late spring afternoon when the getting was good and he thought no one would ever know. And he refrains from trying to justify any part of the havoc his sin has created. He simply says with a heavy heart and a penitent spirit, "I am guilty; I have sinned against the Lord."[17] We would do well to learn from David the character of genuine penitence that God desires.

Presbyterians and Sin

In case you're wondering, Presbyterians are against sin. Traditional Presbyterian beliefs about sin are rooted in such biblical passages as the ones we have just encountered. Of course, these stories do not exist in isolation from the rest of the Bible but are representative of the voice of scripture as a whole. What, then, are the core beliefs about sin to which scripture leads us?

When I was a confirmand in the early 1960s, one of the questions from the Westminster Shorter Catechism that was drilled into me was, "What is sin?" and the answer, "Sin is any want of conformity unto or transgression of the law of God."[18] In other words, *sin is disobeying God by living in contradiction to God's Word in Jesus Christ as he is revealed in scripture.* Here we must tread carefully, lest we find ourselves on the treadmill of legalism by reducing the Bible to a convenient list of rules and regulations. This is one of the dangers we see in the Pharisees' interaction with Jesus. They knew the law of God inside and out, but keeping the letter of the law was more important to many of them than honoring the God who gave the law, so they quickly became the enemies of Jesus. In fact, they used the law as an instrument of self-promotion, which produced, instead of obedience to God, the puffed-up presumption that God would love them because of their spotless record. In other words, the commandments became for them a very serviceable religion, a useful avenue of winning God's favor and congratulating the self. Shirley Guthrie writes,

In relation to God, sin as disobedience is not just being irreligious or breaking the Ten Commandments. Disobedience can also take very pious, religious forms. It is obeying all the commandments, perhaps very strictly, not because we love and trust God but to get something out of God. It is treating our relation to God as a business deal, trying to use God for personal success and happiness (tithing because you get a good return on your investment), or seeking only to save ourselves when we die (see Matt. 16:25).[19]

One day, a Pharisee tried to test Jesus by asking him which commandment is the greatest, and Jesus responded that the entire law is about loving God with all the heart and soul and mind, and loving the neighbor as the self (Matt. 22:34ff.). We somehow need to get it through our heads that the entire purpose of the commandments is *love*, not achieving an impeccable record, not polishing our self-image, not trying to manipulate God into giving us what we want, but *love*. And anything that distorts this purpose is sin; everything that stands in the way of loving God and neighbor selflessly is sin. Being kind to others in order to get a lucky break in return when the chips are down is sin. Being "religious" in order to find a welcome sign at the Pearly Gates is sin. Any use of the commandments that serves a purpose other than unselfish love is sin.

But if sin manifests itself in outward acts of disobedience, *the seed of sin is the rebellion of the heart.* Emil Brunner says it this way: "Sin is defiance, arrogance, the desire to be equal with God. . . ."[20] It is to place ourselves at the center of the universe, assuming (maybe even demanding) that others do the same. Sin is the arrogant attempt to measure ourselves against the sovereign Lord of the universe,[21] the blatant defiance of trying to live on our own terms, assuming that we are masters of our own destiny. In other words, sin means following in the footsteps of Adam and Eve by blurring the line between the Creator and the creature, endeavoring to worship the creature instead of the Creator.

I had a conversation once with a woman whose family had visited our church on several occasions. My hope, of course, was that they were on the verge of joining our congregation but that was the last thing on their minds. She said without the least bit of embarrassment or compunction, "You know, our family does just fine without God; the way we get along in life apparently doesn't have much of anything to do with our religious commitments." And they never came back. Yes, sin is defiance, arrogance, the attempt to live apart from God's reign. Which means that sin also is the arrogance of a pastor or congregation or governing body who thinks it is possible to be the church apart from God's Word—apart from the commandments, apart from the preaching of the great prophets in scripture, apart from the Crucified One who calls us to walk the harder path of self-denial in a feel-good culture and to take up our cross and follow him all the way to Jerusalem, until we dwell at last in the shadow of a mighty cross.

But sin, at its heart, is also a matter of trust, isn't it? This theme is found on almost every page of the Bible. It begins in the wee hours of the first dawn with Adam and Eve and is still glaring at us from the last page of Revelation, as the early church struggles to maintain a living faith in a world where Christians are being fed to the lions. Who is the object of our ultimate trust? Is it ourselves? Human wisdom? Modern science and technology? Our bank account? Our lifestyle? Our family? An enviable education? The precious possessions we treasure? Or is it the God who calls to us across the frontier of life's many uncertainties and tender vulnerabilities and summons us to place our trust in the One who is always faithful and trustworthy and sure? Sin, says Brunner, "is not merely rebellion, it is a kind of dizziness which attacks those who ought to step over the abyss leaning only on God. . . . [It] is composed of the mingled elements of distrust, doubt, and defiant desire for freedom. . . ."[22] At its core, sin is the audacious belief that we can look after ourselves better than God can,[23] so we choose to be autonomous, independent sovereigns rather than dependent creatures who live by the will of God. The story is told of a photo from World War II that pictured a ghetto wall in Warsaw, Poland. A young Jew, apparently struggling with the matter of ultimate trust, had written on the wall, "I believe in the sun, even if it does not shine. I believe in love, even if I do not feel it. I believe in God, even if I do not see God."[24] That is "stepping over the abyss to lean only on God" in the most terrifying nightmare that life can bring. In what or in whom do you trust?

The question of trust brings us squarely to the reality that *sin is idolatry.* In Exodus 32, we find the Israelites impatiently waiting for Moses. God has summoned Moses atop Mount Sinai where he will receive the Ten Commandments on two tablets of stone. Moses, though, is taking far too long to suit the company of Israelites anxiously tapping their collective foot at the bottom of the mountain. They finally grow so exasperated that they gather around Aaron and devise a timely little scheme of their own. If God won't act on their timetable, then they'll create their own god. If God delays in ushering them into the future how and when and where they want, then they'll create their own future. So they say to Aaron, "Come, you be our leader; make gods for us, and we shall worship them." So Aaron orders the people to take off all their gold rings and to bring him every ounce of gold they can find in the camp. He then takes the gold, melts it down, forms it into a mold, casts an image of a calf, and builds an altar before it. When Moses returns from atop the mountain, lo and behold, he finds the Israelites worshiping and sacrificing to the god of their own creation—a golden calf! Whereupon Moses goes into overdrive in order to convince an outraged God not to destroy the entire company of the Israelites.

Idolatry is placing anything other than God in the position of our ultimate loyalty and worship. And if we are totally honest, we all have related rather intimately to the golden calves of our culture. In most Presbyterian congregations, you need only venture as far as the church parking lot on any given Sunday to glimpse one of the golden calves of American affluence. Indeed, the amount of money represented by the handsome array of automobiles, in most instances, far surpasses the annual church budget. Yes, idolatry is a matter of priorities. For others, the golden calf is one's family or job or educational credentials or patriotism. It may be a lovely home or a nice, fat savings account, and for many Presbyterians these days, the golden calf in our lives is maintaining, at the expense of the rest of the world, an affluent standard of living. The story of the golden calf reminds us that *anything* can become an idol if we let it—the dollar, a child, a house, even the Bible or the church.

The refusal to live in community is another way to understand sin. As we see in the creation story, God created us to love and care for one another and to live peaceably with our neighbors. This is God's good purpose for every man, woman, and child on the face of the earth. Why do you suppose racial bigotry leaves an open, bleeding sore on the soul of the human family? Does it have anything to do with the fact that we have forgotten that God made us for each other? Why must God's good earth soak up the blood of brazen hate that justifies so-called ethnic cleansing? And why do more than half of the marriages that begin these days end in broken homes and shattered hearts? Why are children abused or neglected by their parents as though they were no more than expendable commodities in a throw-away culture? Perhaps the answer to all these questions is that we have denied the destiny for which God created us: loving each other within the bonds of community, holding each other up in hardship and suffering, and forgiving the hurt we inevitably inflict on one another.

Why are some of the politicians in our nation's capital driven by greed and power-mongering instead of the noble character and integrity of selfless public service? Why do denominations falter on the edge of schism while their leaders pretend to serve God by finessing their opponents and jockeying for position? And why do you suppose the vast God-given resources of planet Earth are at risk? Why are there so many homeless and hungry people in a world of incredible wealth and affluence and plenty? Maybe we have forgotten that God created us for each other and that, when all is finally said and done, honoring God means taking care of our neighbors.

Another manifestation of our broken relationship with God is a sense of entrapment. Sin means that we are stuck, that what we have done cannot be undone by our own efforts. Our corruption means that no human being can simply make up his or her mind to stop being a sinner. As much as we would like to do away with sin, we are helpless to do so. With Paul we confess,

> I do not understand my own actions. For I do not do what I want, but I do the very thing I hate. . . . I can will what is right, but I cannot do it. For I do not do the good I want, but the evil I do not want is what I do. (Rom. 7:15ff)

This leads us to a rather ominous term that may offend our modern sensibilities: total depravity. As Emil Brunner points out, however, total depravity does not mean that human beings are totally evil and, therefore, incapable of ever making a faithful choice. It means instead that every aspect of human life is corrupted by sin; no part of life is untouched. The nature of sin is such that no one can claim that there are aspects of her or his life that are totally pure, entirely innocent, completely selfless. "The broken relation with God means the perversion and poisoning of all the functions of life. . . ."[25] Even our noblest desires and our most selfless acts are stained by sin. Why? Because we live in a Genesis 3 world where innocence has been lost and pride has worked its deception in the human heart. Because the story of Adam and Eve is the story of every person. Because this is a world where human beings chose to kill the Son of God and to do so in the name of religion on the one hand and justice on the other. And because this is one of the inevitable "givens" in the world into which we were born, a universal reality that we share with all other human beings on the face of the earth. In other words, *this is the question to which Jesus Christ is the answer.* This is the slavery from which we are redeemed. This is the inescapable trap, the original sin, from which Jesus Christ frees us by dying on the cross and rising from the grave.

Finally, as we survey all the manifestations of sin both in ourselves and in the world around us, we face the most tragic reality of all: *The image of God in us is defaced.* When Adam and Eve chose to cross into the forbidden reaches of Eden, the image of God in us was marred so that "the wine of the divine love has become the vinegar of enmity towards God."[26] Indeed, the image of God has not been erased, but that image is now broken, and all humanity will await the One of whom it is written, "He is the visible image of the invisible God, the firstborn of all creation" (Col. 1:15).

A Personal Reflection

Let me venture a personal word at this point, for it is only in translating these concepts into the realm of one's personal life that theology makes any sense at all. My reading of the Bible, my understanding of the Reformed faith, and my experience as a human being have led me to certain convictions about myself as a sinner. Before God and the rest of the human family, I am a sinner—a forgiven sinner, to be sure, but a sinner nonetheless. Without God's grace in Jesus Christ, I am both helpless and hopeless with nothing to look forward to except self-destruction and death. There has never been a moment in my life when I was not a sinner, for I was a sinner in need of God's forgiving love from the moment I was conceived in my mother's womb. Like Paul, I know what is right and I make up my mind that I am going to do the right thing and be the person God wants me to be, but time and time again, I am unable to follow through with it. I can will what is good, but I can't do it by myself. I can desire it, but I am unable to achieve it on my own. So I am blessed to be part of a community that is a hospital for sinners, a community that, week in and week out, gathers to pray,

> Most holy and merciful Father; We acknowledge and confess before Thee;
> Our sinful nature prone to evil and slothful in good; And all our shortcom-
> ings and offenses. Thou alone knowest how often we have sinned; In wan-
> dering from Thy ways; In wasting Thy gifts; In forgetting Thy love. . . .[27]

There is nothing I can do that does not bear the marks of my sinfulness. No matter how hard I try or how much I want to be different, even my purest love for another person carries with it some degree of self-interest on my part. I am incapable of a totally selfless act, or a completely pure thought or word or act or motive, because I am part of a human race that has been flawed, corrupted by sin. Only by the mercy of God can my imperfect love be made whole, and it is, therefore, to the mercy of God that I surrender my life.

Why am I so brutally honest about my sinfulness? There is only one reason: the gospel of Jesus Christ who loves me and gave his life for me. In Christ, my sin does not have dominion over me; for in Christ, I am loved, I am forgiven, and I am granted the grace of God to begin again, to have a fresh start, a clean slate, a new beginning. Because Jesus Christ died on the cross and rose from the grave, sin does not have the last word over me; God does, and it is a word of abundant love and life. We are indeed sinners, but we are *forgiven* sinners who, in each new day, trust the Lord Jesus Christ to forgive our failures, to enable us to forgive each other, and somehow to make our flawed lives redemptive signposts to the living grace of God.[28]

The Wondrous Cross of Salvation

Surely he has borne our infirmities
    and carried our diseases;
yet we accounted him stricken,
    struck down by God, and afflicted.
But he was wounded for our transgressions,
    crushed for our iniquities;
upon him was the punishment that made us whole,
    and by his bruises we are healed.
All we like sheep have gone astray;
    we have all turned to our own way,
and the Lord has laid on him
    the iniquity of us all.

                (Isa. 53:4–6)

While these words of Isaiah originally referred either to the nation of Israel or to an individual servant of the Lord (scholars hold varying views),[29] for two thousand years, the community of the cross has understood Isaiah's words explicitly in relation to Jesus Christ. Our salvation is not the happy by-product of a good man named Jesus, who, as luck would have it, turned out to be a sensational miracle worker, a wise teacher, and a trusted friend of the friendless. No, the salvation of the world is possible only because of the immeasurable sacrifice God was willing to suffer on the cross of Jesus Christ. By *his* bruises, we are healed, and by *his* suffering on the cross, we are saved from death and destruction.

Theologians call this the doctrine of atonement, which focuses the lens of redemption on the reconciliation between God and the human race accomplished in the death of Jesus Christ. For on the old rugged cross two thousand years ago, our broken relationship with God was healed, our alienation overcome, and our estrangement conquered for all eternity. The New Testament portrays God's work of reconciliation through a rich variety of images: the financial image, the military image, the sacrificial image, and the legal image. These images, no doubt, are rather strange to the sensibilities of our modern world. Yet through these images the Bible speaks of our redemption in Christ, and these are the very images of atonement that appear in so many of the great hymns of the church. The fact that the scriptures contain several images suggests that human language literally strains to express the glory of God's triumphant love in Jesus Christ. No single explanation does justice to the One who, dying on the cross, makes all things new. With the help of Professor Shirley Guthrie, we turn now to these various voices within the symphony of scripture.[30]

First is the financial image of the atonement. The scene is a slave market and those present make up a cattle call of human flesh, as they are treated like property and cruelly sold into bondage. Just then, however, the scene turns from one of cruelty to redemption, as one person comes forward and pays the price to purchase the slaves' freedom. In the context of this image, we are the slaves, and Jesus Christ is our gracious Redeemer. "For the Son of Man," says Jesus, "came not to be served but to serve, and to give his life a ransom for many" (Mark 10:45; cf. Rom. 3:24; 1 Cor. 6:20; 7:3; Gal. 3:13; Titus 2:14; and 1 Pet. 1:18).

Next is the military image. Here the action occurs on a battlefield where God and the devil are at war for the possession of the human race. Jesus Christ is God's warrior, who courageously invades the realm of the devil in order to rescue us and bring us safely home again. On Good Friday, Jesus lays down his life in battle, and the devil appears to have won the victory once and for all. But on Easter morning, God raises Jesus from the dead and triumphs eternally over the powers of death, hell, and destruction. The military image surfaces when Paul speaks of a time when Jesus Christ hands over the kingdom to God the Father, having destroyed every ruler and authority and power (1 Cor. 15:24; cf. Col. 1:13; 2:15). And this image of the atonement has been etched in our hearts by Martin Luther's great Reformation hymn, "A Mighty Fortress Is Our God":

> And though this world, with devils filled,
> Should threaten to undo us,
> We will not fear, for God hath willed
> His truth to triumph through us.
> The prince of darkness grim, we tremble not for him;
> His rage we can endure, For lo! His doom is sure,
> One little word shall fell him.[31]

Then there is the sacrificial image. Now we find ourselves in a place of sacred worship where sacrifices are being offered to atone for the sins of the people. In this scenario, we are the guilty who deserve God's condemnation, but the very moment we are poised to offer our sacrifices of atonement, a priest comes forward and acts as the mediator between God and us. The priest's sacrifice, however, is entirely different from all other sacrifices ever made. Instead of offering an animal sacrifice, he offers his own life as an act of saving love and, in doing so, makes the one definitive sacrifice that accomplishes, for all eternity, reconciliation between God and the human race. Jesus Christ is the priest who makes atonement for our sins by offering up his life on the cross. The book of Hebrews says it with these words:

> Since, then, we have a great high priest who has passed through the heavens, Jesus, the Son of God, let us hold fast to our confession. For we do not

have a high priest who is unable to sympathize with our weakness, but we have one who in every respect has been tested as we are, yet without sin. Let us therefore approach the throne of grace with boldness, so that we may receive mercy and find grace to help in time of need. (4:14–16)

Likewise, Paul speaks of "the redemption that is in Christ Jesus, whom God put forward as a sacrifice of atonement by his blood, effective through faith" (Rom. 3:22a–25a; cf. Mark 14:22–24; John 1:29; 1 Cor. 5:7).

Last, we come to the legal image of the atonement. As the curtain goes up, we are in a court of law where God, the just Judge, has summoned the human race to the bar of justice to stand trial for the sins of hatred and rebellion. The divine law has been broken, and justice will now be executed. The verdict is announced: Guilty. And the sentence is given: Death. But just as the sentence is about to be carried out, a righteous person who has obeyed the law perfectly and is entirely without sin comes forward and takes the death sentence upon himself, suffering all the consequences of human sin and guilt. The enemies of God are now acquitted. The slate is wiped clean, and we are free to begin a new life. In the words of Paul:

What then are we to say about these things? If God is for us, who is against us? He who did not withhold his own Son, but gave him up for all of us, will he not with him also give us everything else? Who will bring any charge against God's elect? It is God who justifies. Who is to condemn? It is Christ Jesus, who died, yes, who was raised, who is at the right hand of God, who indeed intercedes for us. (Rom. 8:31–34; cf. Rom. 5:6–11; 2 Cor. 5:16–21; Col. 1:19–20)

These scenes seem remarkably out of step with the alluring images of our modern world, where Madison Avenue knows how to pack a wallop and sell a product. There are even voices today inside the church that question whether the traditional language of atonement is meaningful at all for modern, educated people who live in a sophisticated world. Several years ago at a widely publicized conference, one of the speakers said, "I don't think we need a theory of atonement at all. I don't think we need folks hanging on crosses and blood dripping and weird stuff."[32]

Whether or not the cross seems "weird" in our culture, as if we are the standard-bearers, is not the issue. In fact, the cross has always seemed "weird" to the world. Human societies typically do not look to a dying figure nailed to a tree for divine revelation, which is the very reason Paul wrote to the Corinthians: "For Jews demand signs and Greeks desire wisdom, but we proclaim Christ crucified, a stumbling block to Jews and foolishness to Gentiles . . ." (1 Cor. 1:22–23). Without the cross there is no Christian faith. The cross of Jesus Christ is absolutely central to the faith of the church, and every effort to replace it with more sophisticated, user-friendly images of salvation is nothing more than a flagrant attempt to define God according to our personal tastes and aesthetic temperaments (perhaps a golden calf is what we need). Indeed, "the message about the cross is foolishness to those who are perishing, but to us who are being saved it is the power of God" (1 Cor. 1:18). The cross is at the heart of everything that Christ calls us to be and to do, and living a life faithful to God is utterly inconceivable apart from the atoning sacrifice of Christ on the cross. In the words of Jürgen Moltmann: "The death of Jesus on the cross is the *centre* of all Christian theology. . . . All Christian statements about God, about creation, about sin and death have their focal point in the crucified Christ."[33]

The cross may not be the way that you and I would have chosen to redeem the world, but it is unquestionably the way God chose, and the marvelous thing is that all four images of atonement strain with all the power of human language to declare the same central truth: We humans are trapped in the predicament of sin, death, and destruction from which we are totally helpless to free ourselves, and God, at the cost of great personal sacrifice, becomes a human being in Jesus Christ to do for us the very thing we are incapable of doing for ourselves—forgive our sins, heal our broken relationship with God and each other, and restore our hope for the future. Moreover, it is the *injured* party, not the guilty party, who reaches out in love to create reconciliation. The One whose love has been rejected bears full responsibility for the evil that plagues this weary world and holds human life in the grip of pride and rebellion.

The grace of God is finally beyond all human comprehension, but in Jesus Christ God has identified with us in every way imaginable and has assumed all our frailty, all our rebellion, all our brokenness, all our lies, all our murderously inhuman ways toward each other. Jesus Christ bore in his body on the cross the terror and hatred and horrific destruction of the ages. And, because of Christ's sacrifice, we are assured that the horrors of terrorism and the silent but deadly ache of broken hearts will not have the last word over us. For God has personally made eternal peace with us. These are the unfathomable depths of God's love. The Judge loves us so much that he is willing to be judged in our place. Indeed, "God proves his love for us in that while we still were sinners Christ died for us" (Rom. 5:8).

"Death has been swallowed up in victory." (1 Cor. 15:54)

The death of Jesus on Good Friday, however, is not the end of the story of salvation. The foundation of the Christian faith is not only the suffering of Jesus Christ on the cross but also the endless alleluias of Easter. No human language can even approximate God's "indescribable gift" (2 Cor. 9:15), but on Easter morning God raised Jesus from the grave, thereby conquering the powers of evil once and for all. Christ is risen! Death is dead![34] Evil has been vanquished! On Easter morning, Christ's lifeless clump of dead flesh, by the power of God, got up and lived again. And because he lives, we, too, shall live (John 14:19).

Easter, however, does not begin with sounding trumpets and soaring melodies but in the heart of suffering and despair. It's a familiar place where we all have been at some point in our lives, a place where some of us no doubt are living at this very moment. The name of the place is Heartbreak, and that's where our risen Lord has planted the seeds of resurrection. Easter begins at Heartbreak where wounded human beings face the dead end of broken hearts and crushed spirits. Easter begins at Heartbreak because this is precisely where the risen Christ enters our lives—in the midst of that struggle and in the ache of boundless night.

A young woman comes home from work one day only to find that her husband has spent the last several hours packing because he is about to move out. It comes like a bolt out of the blue. She had no earthly idea that he was so unhappy. From her perspective, the marriage was strong. Their union was solid, secure. But in the late afternoon shadows, she hears those heartbreaking words come out of his mouth: "I don't love you anymore; I have found someone else."

A teenager comes home from school in tears. When his parents finally get him to open up, they learn that he doesn't have any friends. The high school scene is simply a gigantic network of cliques, and he doesn't fit into any of them. "If only I could look into the mirror and like what I see," he says to his parents amid the sobs of self-loathing and regret.

Someone else makes it to middle age only to find herself sinking into the depths of depression. She doesn't understand why, but she is plagued by a deep, unshakable sadness—a sadness so consuming that she can't even get out of bed most mornings. Finally, through conversation with a therapist, she learns that she is simply replaying mental tapes from her childhood, and the monsters from the past are hunting her down.

This is Heartbreak. This is where Easter begins. The resurrection of Jesus Christ is for people who struggle to find meaning in the muddled mess of the past they have created, who are gripped by fear deep in the pits of their stomachs as they face the agonizing realities of today, and who wonder how in God's good name they can ever face the painful uncertainties of tomorrow. The good news of Easter is that, in the face of the most insufferable hardships and outrageous terrors that life can bring, death is conquered, evil is defeated, and all creation is invited to join Paul in mocking death:

"Death has been swallowed up in victory."
"Where, O death, is your victory?
Where, O death is your sting?"

The sting of death is sin, and the power of sin is the law. But thanks be to God, who gives us the victory through our Lord Jesus Christ. (1 Cor. 15:54–57)

When the hardships of life beat us down and the dawn of each new day seems to promise a double measure of despair, the good cheer of the gospel is that sin has been beaten, the curse has been conquered. We still face the silent agonies of the heart, but of one thing we are certain: The victory has been won, and Jesus Christ is the Victor! On any given day, it may not feel like it, but the resurrection of Jesus Christ is an eternal victory that is both *already* and *not yet*:

Easter is indeed the great pledge of our hope, but simultaneously this future is already present in the Easter message. It is the proclamation of a victory already won. The war is at an end—even though here and there troops are still shooting, because they have not heard anything yet about the capitulation. . . . It is in this interim space that we are living. . . . The Easter message tells us that our enemies, sin, the curse and death, are beaten. Ultimately they can no longer start mischief. They still behave as though the game were not decided, the battle not fought; we must still reckon with them, but fundamentally we must cease to fear them any more.[35]

This is the good news that is ours to tell—the church's treasure of joy that we have been called to share with all creation. David H. C. Read once preached a sermon entitled "Unfinished Easter."[36] I have always been intrigued by the title, because Easter is indeed unfinished in the sense that the final chapter of the Easter story has yet to be written in the days and weeks and months and years of our lives. What will the chapter say that you are writing with your life? Will it be the story of despair and bitterness? Or will it be the story of the living, risen Christ?

Truth 4

God's Love Is Not for Sale

For by grace you have been saved through faith, and this is not your own doing; it is the gift of God—not the result of works, so that no one may boast.

(Eph. 2:8–9)

God Helps Those Who Help Themselves?

Picture it. You've got your TV remote control in your hand and you're channel surfing when you just happen to land on a televangelist who really has his shorts in a knot. As the heat of passion rises, the entire auditorium becomes electric with emotion. Finally, the climax of the service arrives, and the preacher calls for a personal decision for Jesus Christ. He says with a sincere, imploring tone in his voice, "Turn to God in faith, confess your sins, and God will love you and accept you into his kingdom."

I hope by now that your theological antenna is telling you that something is terribly wrong with that scene—not the fever pitch emotionalism, but the message, the content. That televangelist has turned faith itself into a work. He has said that *if* we want God to be gracious to us, then the ball is in our court and all we have to do is turn to God and have faith; *if* we want God to love us, then we'd better repent and confess our sins. Quite to the contrary, however, the gospel of Jesus Christ offers an entirely different message. It says, "God is a benevolent God who already loves us; in fact, God loves us so much that Jesus Christ died on the cross for our sins. And because God is gracious, we are free to turn to him, repent of our sins, and begin a faithful life of gratitude before God."

Do you see the difference? In the first instance, we elevate ourselves to the status of God's partner in salvation to the point where we ourselves are partially responsible for saving our own necks. God accomplishes the divine part of our salvation, then we accomplish the human part, and only then is salvation a fait accompli. In this view, salvation,

84

in the final analysis, is up to us. God has thrown the ball into our court and is waiting to see if we will come to our senses, have faith, and turn to God. But biblical faith will have none of this. The gospel of Jesus Christ, from start to finish, is the unmitigated good news of God's unconditional grace. In the words of Calvin's famous hymn:

> Our hope is in no other save in Thee;
> Our faith is built upon Thy promise free. . . .[1]

This may be the hardest part of all Christian truth for us to hear. When I was a child, my surrounding culture taught me at an early age that I had better get busy and do something with my life because "God helps those who help themselves." But that axiom, touted by many to be a direct quote from the Bible, is as unbiblical as any statement could be. *The good news of Jesus Christ is that God does for us precisely what we are totally unable to do for ourselves. Our faith, indeed, "is built upon Thy promise free."* Our faith is not in our ability to pull ourselves up by the bootstraps, or in our sound judgment and keen insight, given all available choices, to choose God. In truth, human sin renders us *incapable* of choosing God, so God chooses us, God breaks into our lives with divine grace, God thaws our cold hearts by the passionate fire of the Holy Spirit. Our faith is in God's totally free and gracious benevolence toward us. We are able to turn to God only because God first turned to us in Jesus Christ. "We love because he first loved us" (1 John 4:19), and the full weight of the Bible stands over against any and every effort to turn faith into a work. Indeed, God's love is not for sale.

We need to be careful not to confuse this discussion with Christ's call to live out our faith courageously and faithfully through costly acts of love (we'll come to that in the next chapter). Rather, this is about what makes a relationship with God possible in the first place. Traditionally, theologians have called this the doctrine of justification by grace through faith, meaning that we are justified before God (or made right with God) not by anything we do or achieve through our own efforts but purely by the grace of God in loving us and forgiving the sin that separates us. This belief, which is central to all Protestant theology, provided the spark for the Protestant Reformation in the sixteenth century, and one of the best ways to understand it is through the life of Martin Luther.

Martin Luther
and the Beginning of the Reformation

Martin Luther was a man tormented by doubts about his relationship with God. He knew God to be holy and righteous, and he knew himself to be a wretched sinner who fell miserably short of the holiness demanded by a righteous God and who deserved only the wrath of God's condemnation. The question that plagued Luther was the same question that drove him first into the pit of despair and later into the eye of the Reformation's storm: "How can I, sinner that I am, possibly have a relationship with God?"

Luther was born in Eisleben, Germany, in 1483 to peasant parents who had high hopes for their son's future. Shortly after his birth, the family moved to Mansfeld where Luther's father became determined to provide an education that would properly prepare his son for a career in law. But when Luther graduated in 1505 as a master of arts, his life took a dramatic turn away from law and toward a full-time spiritual quest. A driving force in Luther's life was a deep sense of his personal sinfulness and an inescapable guilt resulting from it. So in July of 1505, he entered a monastery of Augustinian hermits in Erfurt where he hoped to enter so fully into the religious life that his guilt and sin would be overcome and he would prove himself worthy of God's love. Luther was a man of many gifts, and he quickly won recognition from his superiors. He was ordained to the priesthood in 1507 and was soon sent to Wittenberg to prepare for a university professorship. After graduating as a bachelor of theology in 1509, his scholarly endeavors paved the way to a doctorate in theology in 1512, whereupon he began to teach the Bible extensively. As a preacher and teacher, Luther's gifts were so well recognized that he was appointed director of studies in his own cloister, as well as district vicar. Luther excelled in every endeavor that he undertook and "bore the repute of a man of singular piety, devotion, and monastic zeal."[2] But for all the status and success he had so ably achieved, Luther remained bereft of grace and felt that he lived in the grip of condemnation. The harder he tried to prove his worth before God, the more spiritually desolate Luther felt. Little did he know that his life was poised to take another dramatic turn that would change the course of history.

According to Luther's own account, his theological breakthrough occurred as a new understanding of the righteousness of God was born within him, an understanding rooted in the extravagant grace of God to forgive sinners with unconditional love. It was a gradual dawning of the truth, but it was a truth that would eventually shake the very foundation of Luther's soul, grant him the blessed peace for which he had long hungered, and, in turn, make him the adversary of the sixteenth-century religious establishment. The *only* thing that saves us, said Luther, is the grace of God—the pure, unqualified, unmitigated grace of God. In fact, it is entirely impossible for any person, no matter how accomplished or intelligent or well-meaning or "religious," to win God's favor by good deeds. The monk in the monastery cannot do it; the hard-working businessperson cannot do it; the compassionate pastor cannot do it; the nurturing homemaker cannot do it; the self-giving parent cannot do it; the obedient son or daughter cannot do it; the morality-driven special-interest group cannot do it; *no human being can do it*. We are justified before God only because of God's gracious disposition toward us.

Luther, however, was convinced that the church of his day perverted the gospel by emphasizing good works as an avenue to salvation. In particular, Luther objected to the sale of indulgences through which the church conveniently fattened the church's treasury by forgiving the penalties of sin. Luther found this practice to be, in a word, blasphemous. So on October 31, 1517, Luther nailed his Ninety-five Theses to the door of the castle church in Wittenberg. They were ninety-five reasons that the church needed renewal and were intended primarily to engender discussion and reform. Luther, however, soon found himself embroiled in a controversy of mammoth proportions, the outcome of which would not only change Luther's life but the whole of the church.

A Theology of Beggars:
Grace Comes before Faith

Douglas John Hall has set the controversy sparked by Luther's insistence on divine grace as the sole source of salvation in terms of a theology of beggars, taken directly from the leaves of Luther's writing. In 1515, as the truth first began to dawn in Luther's soul, he preached a sermon in which he said, "Preach one thing: the wisdom of the cross."[3] Then shortly before his death thirty-one years later, the last words ever penned by Luther were these: "We are beggars, that's true."[4] Hall observes the essential unity between these two statements, one from a young pastor and the other from a learned reformer:

> To confess "the wisdom of the cross" means, at the most existential level, to know oneself devoid of wisdom. It means being a beggar where understanding is concerned—where life itself is concerned. The gospel of the cross condemns every pretension to possession. It divests man of all he has attempted to use to cover up his essential nakedness. It reduces him to the status of a beggar, robbed, beaten, and naked at the side of the road. Only a beggar can receive the gift of grace. Moreover, he must become a beggar again and again. His natural tendency is to regard himself as self-sufficient, autonomous, master of the situation. Even the man of faith—he especially—falls into this habit. He turns faith itself into the stuff that will elevate him above the beggarly condition. He regards himself as growing progressively beyond his beggarly condition. . . . At the end as at the beginning, "we are beggars."[5]

A theology of beggars is probably not the most popular sermon topic or Sunday school theme for middle- and upper-middle-class American Presbyterians who pride themselves on attaining a station in life far, far removed from any identity even remotely resembling a beggar. We prefer to think of ourselves as movers and shakers, takers and doers, arrangers and managers—anything but beggars. But Luther reminds us that, in the deep recesses of the human heart, that is exactly what we are, because even the wealthiest and most accomplished among us stand totally naked and vulnerable before the throne of God, and to presume to be otherwise is not only wrong-headed, but blasphemous. The gospel of Jesus Christ is built on a grace that is so extravagant that it is beyond all human powers of comprehension. A relationship with God is a *free gift*, pure and simple (cf. Rom. 5:15–17). There is not one thing that any person, even the kindest and noblest, can ever do to attain it, because even the kindest and noblest lives are corrupted by sin, which casts every human being who ever walks the face of the earth into the role of a beggar who can only receive God's grace, not win it or earn it or buy it. According to Karl Barth,

> "Justification by faith" cannot mean that instead of his customary evil works and in place of all kinds of supposed good works man chooses and accomplishes the work of faith, in this way pardoning and therefore justifying himself. . . . Even in the action of faith he is the sinful man who as such is not in a position to justify himself, who with every attempt to justify himself can only become more deeply entangled in his sin. . . . If his faith is his justification, his pardon, . . . he does not owe this in the very least to what he is and feels and thinks and says and does as a believing person. . . . Faith is not at all the supreme and true and finally successful form of self-justification.[6]

A theology of beggars, therefore, asks us to reckon with one of the most difficult of all Christian truths: In a culture of consumption where the wheels of progress are judged by a ledger sheet of sales and profits and in which most Presbyterians check the day's trading on Wall Street with greater interest than they examine their souls, God's love is not for sale. The heart of the gospel is that *God's grace comes before our faith.*[7] Our faith is not in our faith. Our faith is not in our ability to consider all possible options and end up choosing God. Our faith is not in the rightness of our theological judgment, whether it be labeled liberal or conservative or open-minded or inclusive or anything else. Our faith is not in the morality we profess or the pretense of high ethical standards we maintain or the Bible we read. Our faith is not in a pristine sexual ethic or a blameless record in keeping the standards of biblical morality. Our faith is not in anything we can do to make ourselves look a little better and thereby acceptable to God. Rather, our faith is in the totally amazing grace of God "to save a wretch like me," and the only hope the gospel offers the world is rooted in "Thy promise free." As Paul tells the congregation in Rome, "But God proves his love for us in that while we still were sinners Christ died for us" (Rom. 5:8)—not after we pulled ourselves up by the bootstraps and did a splendid job of helping ourselves, *but while we were totally helpless to save ourselves.*

The Outlandishly Extravagant Grace of God

Who knows? Maybe it's the Protestant work ethic that has ingrained in us the belief that we only get out of life what we put in. Of course, this is true in many circumstances of life. In a person's vocation, for example, one can rightly expect only to reap the rewards of hard work and diligent effort, and, in the absence of such, there will be a meager return on a meager investment. All of the easy jobs seem to have been given to someone else, and most of us have learned the hard-knocks lesson of life that there are no free rides. Or take the case of marriage, as well as the parent-child relationship. Chances are, if one doesn't make a substantive investment of love, devotion, and time in one's spouse and children, there will be little or nothing in the way of a meaningful, enduring relationship. Successful marriages do not just happen, and neither do redemptive relationships between parents and children. To a large degree, of course, the same is true of the Christian life. The satisfactions and fulfillment of discipleship to Jesus Christ arise, in part, through the dedicated commitment to live as a disciple. But once again, the concern of this chapter is not how a person lives out the Christian life, but what makes a relationship with God possible in the first place. And a theological problem of gargantuan proportions surfaces the moment we attempt to base a relationship with God on anything but the outlandishly extravagant grace of God.

God tells the Israelites in the book of Deuteronomy:

> It was not because you were more numerous than any other people that the LORD set his heart on you and chose you—for you were the fewest of all peoples. It was because the LORD loved you and kept the oath that he swore to your ancestors, that the LORD has brought you out with a mighty hand, and redeemed you from the house of slavery. . . . (Deut. 7:7–8)

The Israelites did nothing—a big fat zero—to warrant God's favor. Their relationship with God wasn't based on anything they had done or believed or hoped or dreamed. When God called Abraham and Sarah, they were part of a landless class of people with no son and, therefore, no future. And by the time

Moses appeared on the scene, the only distinction of the Hebrew people was their despair of slavery under Pharaoh and their cries for redemption and release. They were in a position only to receive, not to take or achieve anything on their own.

Consider also the parable of the Laborers in the Vineyard in Matthew 20:1–16. Here Jesus seizes every attempt at self-justification and throws it in the garbage heap of human scorekeeping. A certain landowner went out first thing in the morning to hire laborers for the day. After discussing the day's wage, off they went to earn their keep. Later that morning, the landowner returned to the marketplace only to find laborers who had not been hired, so he promptly loaded them up as well and sent them out to labor in his vineyard. He then did the same thing at noon, at three o'clock, and at five o'clock.

When evening came, it was time to settle up with the workers, and the landowner decided to start with those who were hired last. They came forward not knowing exactly what to expect but were delighted to see that the landowner was kind enough to pay them a full day's wage. "What a bonanza!" all the others thought, as their hearts palpitated with sheer exhilaration over the windfall that was suddenly staring them in the face. But the landowner stunned them all by paying each one exactly the same as the five o'clock workers—a full day's wage, no more, no less.

"This has got to be a joke!" lamented those who had worked all day. "We showed up on your stinking plot of land and worked our fingers to the bone for twelve solid hours. Look at this sunburn we got from the scorching sun! We didn't even take all the breaks we were entitled to. Now our backs are aching, our feet are sore, we're thirsty, and this isn't even enough money to buy a couple of cold ones!"

But the landowner is completely undeterred in his decision to pay everyone equally. "Watch it, buster;[8] you're treading on thin ice. You agreed to work all day for a day's wage. Right? Right. And have I paid you as promised and on schedule? All right, then, get over yourself, because what I pay the others is none of your business. Maybe the real problem here is that you're just plain green with envy because I'm generous!"

That, in a nutshell, is the entire point. God is generous. The gospel is unqualified good news because God is inherently gracious toward us, and our lives are made right with God because and only because of God's generous disposition.[9] God loves us with the love that gives us precisely what we don't deserve and haven't merited and can never ever in a million years achieve on our own. God is eternally for us. God's love is unconditional. The grace of God contains no "ifs." And this is the God who is "the great fact," who sent Jesus Christ to die for us *while we were yet sinners*. The parable of the Laborers in the Vineyard is one of many illustrations in the Bible of God's *No* to every human attempt at self-justification. And only upon hearing God's *No* can we hear God's eternal *Yes* in Jesus Christ.

This is not a very palatable story to those who are into scorekeeping as a way of life and to those whose lives are relentlessly driven by balance sheets, rewards, and punishment. And, frankly, it is more than a little audacious of Jesus to tell this story in such impeccably "religious" company. Robert Farrar Capon writes,

> Bookkeeping is the only punishable offense in the kingdom of heaven. For in that happy state, the *books* are ignored forever, and there is only the *Book* of life. And in that book, nothing stands against you. There are no debit entries that can keep you out of the clutches of the Love that will not let you go. There is no minimum balance below which the grace that finagles all accounts will cancel your credit. And there is, of course, no need for you to show large amounts of black ink, because the only Auditor before whom you must finally stand is the Lamb—and he has gone deaf, dumb, and blind on the cross.[10]

Free to Choose?

One of the most famous heresies in the history of the church blazed to the surface through a man named Pelagius, a British monk who began to teach in Rome about the year 400. Pelagius was a staunch advocate of the freedom of the human will, insisting that "If I ought, I can," and his views sparked a theological row that pitted Pelagius against St. Augustine.[11] Shirley Guthrie characterizes Pelagianism in this way:

> This position argues that God has given us laws and commandments to tell us how we must live, and the freedom to obey or disobey them. If we choose to obey, God will be gracious to us and will help and save us; if we refuse to obey we will get the rejection and punishment we deserve. In other words, we save (or damn) ourselves by the "good works" we do (or refuse to do).[12]

In other words, Pelagius insisted that we humans have the innate ability both to choose what is good and to act upon our good choice. Personal salvation then becomes a matter of making the right choice and—lucky us!—we hit the jackpot and get elevated to the status of coauthor of our own salvation simply by giving one right answer.

Now, if this seems a bit extreme on the side of positive thinking with regard to human nature, then never you fear, because there arose a more moderate form of Pelagianism known as semi-Pelagianism (don't laugh; I have a hunch there are people all over the church who think this cinches their deal with God). This view was spawned by followers of Pelagius who did not deny the need for God's grace but believed that the first steps toward salvation are taken by the human being[13] and that grace enters the picture later, helping us, in a sense, to finish what we were able on our own steam to begin. Once more, we turn to Shirley Guthrie who captures the spirit of semi-Pelagianism:

> We are all unworthy, undeserving sinners. We not only leave undone many things we ought to have done; even the good we do is corrupted by sinful motives, desires, and goals. We are totally dependent on the saving grace of God in Jesus Christ for our salvation. But although it is true that we are not free and able to save ourselves by our good works, we are free and able to do one thing. We can acknowledge our *need* for God's grace and turn to God to *ask* for the deep, abiding faith, hope, and love we cannot achieve for ourselves. We can confess Christ as Lord and Savior and show our willingness to *receive* the salvation made available to us in him. We can *allow* the transforming power of God's Holy Spirit to come into our hearts. We can go to church in order to express our *desire* for the help and salvation we know comes only from God. . . . And if we choose God and turn to God in this way, God will choose us, love, help, and save us. . . . Salvation is by God's grace alone, available to all who sincerely ask for it and want it.[14]

As you can see, semi-Pelagianism is a nifty little adventure in divine-human cooperation. God does the divine part of salvation, you and I do our part, and everyone lives happily ever after. And as I have suggested, semi-Pelagianism is alive and well in the church today. It springs to life whenever a person attempts to live by the slogan "God helps those who help themselves" and each time some well-meaning soul trumpets the promise "Turn to God, have faith in Jesus Christ, and you will be saved." It arises whenever people think they have to *do* something or *think* and *act* in a certain way in order to make the salvation of God effective in their lives.

But the sin in our lives does not amount to a few unfortunate indiscretions into which the circumstances of the moment pushed us. Sin is the condition in which we are "prone to evil and slothful in good." Ours is a predicament so dire that even our finest motives and highest ideals and brightest hopes and purest loves are corrupted by the self-interest of a handsome payback. Yes, the ocean of sin is so deep and treacherous that no mere mortal can cross it and live. The entrapment of sin is much more serious than a momentary impairment of our faculties of judgment, and it can never be reduced to a minor bump in the road when in actual fact it is a dead end of self-destruction from which we can only cry out to God for redemption. So let us face up to the truth once and for all: *Sin means that we have lost the freedom to choose God.* That is one choice that only God can make for us and in us. And this is why God became a human being in Jesus Christ—to do for us the very thing we are helpless to do for ourselves, to rescue us from self-destruction and set right our relationship with God and neighbor.

Looking to Jesus Christ Alone

What, then, do we contribute to our salvation? Nothing. Absolutely nothing, because we are a community of beggars. Look at Calvary. It is a dark day in human history, as the shadows of evil cast an ominous haze of doom over all creation. Outside the city wall of Jerusalem, the wheels of human justice triumphantly turn, as a crowd of curiosity seekers gazes at three convicted criminals being crucified—getting their just deserts, as it were. A man named Jesus is dying on the cross in the middle, between two sleazy thugs. That is the company the Savior of the world keeps as he goes forth to storm the gates of hell and vanquish the powers of evil. Just then, Jesus gasps for the breath that is slowly being squeezed from his mortal body and, in desolation, he screams a scream that still sears the human heart, "My God, my God, why have you forsaken me?" It is a moment of terrifying agony, as all the sin and rebellion of the entire human race descends with lethal power on the soul of the godforsaken One. And suddenly we know that Jesus Christ has descended into hell to pay for our sins, and that all the centuries of self-justification have met their merciful end in him. It is the final and eternal *No* of God to every futile attempt to win divine favor and, in the same moment, it is the eternal and exquisitely gracious *Yes* of God to our lives in Jesus Christ. Therefore,

> The believer looks to Him [Jesus Christ] and in Him to himself and his fellow-man of every age and clime, both near and distant, to find in Him their righteousness before God, their yesterday and tomorrow, their end, their beginning, their pardon, their peace with God. . . . Faith ceases to be faith . . . if it looks anywhere but to Him, if the believer tries to look at himself and to rely and trust on his own activity and accomplishment. . . . Everything depends on the fact that it [faith] is being in encounter with the living Jesus Christ.[15]

So what do you and I contribute to our salvation? Look again at the dying One hanging on the cross. What contribution did any human being make to that scene on Calvary? Only one contribution, yours and mine: sin. As William Temple has written, "All is of God; the only thing of my own which I can contribute to my own redemption is the sin from which I need to be redeemed. . . ."[16]

Faith As an Empty Vessel

What then is faith? Is it not a personal act on my part? And is it not also a free and willing decision to follow Jesus Christ in life and in death? *Of course,* faith is a deeply personal act, but before it is my act, it is God's gift to me, and only because it is first God's gift can it then become my personal act of faith. And, *of course,* faith is the free and willing decision to be obedient to Jesus Christ, but our obedience is anchored purely in Christ's obedience. The free and willing decision that I make is a *response,* a response of gratitude for the "love so amazing, so divine," that it "demands my soul, my life, my all."[17] Faith, therefore, is the life of humble obedience on which I have embarked with the empty hands of a beggar. For this reason, John Calvin says, "We compare faith to a kind of vessel; for unless we come empty and with the mouth of our soul open to seek Christ's grace, we are not capable of receiving Christ."[18] Karl Barth echoes Calvin's thought:

> For because it is faith in Jesus Christ, . . . it has to be an empty hand, an empty vessel, a vacuum. It can be said of the believer at all times and in all circumstances: "What hast thou that thou didst not receive?" (I Cor. 4[7]), and: "By the grace of God I am what I am" (I Cor. 15[10]).[19]

What are we, indeed, by the grace of God? *Forgiven* sinners. Faith breaks into our lives as sheer grace, pure miracle, empowering us to acknowledge Jesus Christ as Lord and Savior and, in doing so, to fall to our knees in unspeakable gratitude. God is eternally for us, so we no longer have to try and earn God's favor. With gratitude, we can say to each other with abiding faith, *"Friends, believe the good news of the gospel. In Jesus Christ we are forgiven. Thanks be to God!"*

Truth 5

God Gives New Life

So if anyone is in Christ, there is a new creation: everything old has passed away; see, everything has become new!

(2 Cor. 5:17)

After Forgiveness, What Next?

A young man named Ian is the hero of Anne Tyler's novel *Saint Maybe*. As the curtain goes up, Ian is a high school student who possesses the perfect combination of intelligence and affability. With a steady girlfriend and all the right "stuff," Ian's future appears to be bright with promise.

But one night, Ian confronts his growing suspicion that Lucy, the wife of his brother, Danny, has been unfaithful. Ian feels that Danny is blind to Lucy's deceit and that he needs to wake up and face the facts. So one night, sitting outside the house in Danny's Chevy, Ian tells Danny about his suspicion. Afterwards, when Ian goes into the house, Danny remains alone in the car, and the next thing Ian knows, the scene has spun out of control. He hears the Chevy's engine roaring. As he pulls back the curtain, Ian sees the headlights swinging abruptly away from the curb, and as Danny begins to peel rubber, Ian drops the curtain to shield himself from the terror in the street that is about to change his life forever. A moment later, Danny crashes into a stone wall at the end of the block and dies.

In the wake of Danny's tragedy, Ian is awash with guilt. He is convinced that Danny drove his Chevy into the stone wall because of the devastation he felt after hearing Ian's suspicion, and that meant only one thing to Ian: It was his fault. Not long afterwards, Danny's wife, Lucy, also dies, leaving behind three small children. What would Ian do with all the tragic pieces of his family's life? How could he deal with the relentless guilt and gnawing ache in his soul?

95

Strangely enough, Ian finds the answer to his pain in the Church of the Second Chance. Mind you, this is totally unlike any experience of "church" known to Ian and is dissimilar in almost every way from the Dober Street Presbyterian Church where Ian's family belongs. Yet by some strange miracle of grace, Ian hears God speak to him in the fellowship of this small congregation, and the message he hears is that God wants him to take care of Danny and Lucy's three children. So Ian leaves college, closes the door forever on the bright future that everyone believes is his destiny, and devotes his life to caring for the children whose lives had been struck not with one, but two tragedies. Everyone thinks he has totally lost it—his parents, his friends, his girlfriend. "What are you, crazy?" one of his friends asks him. "You've got a life to live! You can't drag [these kids] around with you forever." Ian's parents, though, are perhaps the most disturbed of all. "Ian, have you fallen into the hands of some *sect*?" his father demands.

"No, I haven't," Ian responds. "I have merely discovered a church that makes sense to me, the same as Dober Street Presbyterian makes sense to you and Mom."

"Dober Street didn't ask us to abandon our educations," his mother protests. "Of course we have nothing against religion; we raised all you children to be Christians. But *our* church never asked us to abandon our entire way of life." Danny, however, has heard the voice of God, and despite all the pressure to the contrary, he remains undeterred in his pursuit of obedience.[1]

That is the subject of this chapter: the pursuit of obedience even when the gospel demands that we abandon our old way of life and willingly embrace the new life to which God calls us. From the moment we fall to our knees in gratitude for the unspeakably gracious gift of forgiveness, a whole new future opens up, as we yield our lives to God and ask God to tame every desire of the heart.[2] Like Ian, embracing the new life to which God calls us may mean turning our backs on old ways of doing things, even on old relationships. When God begins to tame the desires of our hearts, those around us may grow uncomfortable with the changes, and some, no doubt, will think, as did Ian's friends and parents, that we have taken leave of our senses. After all, we want a loving God who forgives us but doesn't change us. We prefer a God who comforts us but doesn't challenge the intimate details of our lives. We want to feel secure in the arms of Jesus, not vulnerable to the fresh winds of the Holy Spirit. But the good news of the gospel is that, in forgiving our sins, *God gives us new life*, and the security of resting in the arms of Jesus and the perils of being vulnerable to the fresh winds of the Holy Spirit go hand in hand. It is impossible to have one without the other.

According to an account by William Willimon, Stanley Hauerwas often opens one of his classes at Duke University by reading a letter from a concerned parent to a government official. The parent has evidently done everything possible to prepare his son for the brightest future imaginable, providing the best education money could buy. And just, it seems, as this young man is headed toward a good job as a lawyer, he gets involved in some kooky religious sect, and the parent writes to a government official, complaining about the intrusion of this sect into the life of his son. The parent levels a staunch protest against the sect for influencing his son's every move, telling him whom it is appropriate to date and whom it is not, and even having the audacity to assume responsibility for his son's use of money.

"Whom is this letter describing?" Hauerwas then asks his class, and they inevitably come up with all manner of weird sects. Then Hauerwas reveals that it is a composite letter drawn from several third-century letters from Roman parents who are complaining about the demands of a group called the church.[3]

It staggers the imagination—doesn't it?—that anyone would consider the church a subversive community. That is, it staggers the imagination of twenty-first-century, affluent Americans who have no intention of letting their religion get in the way of everything that made them affluent Americans to start with—their relation to money, to family, to work, to a certain political persuasion, to national pride, and to the profiteering values inherent in a system where the rich get richer and the poor get poorer. *But the truth is, God gives new life!* The love of God *changes* us. The grace of God *re-creates* us. And being a disciple of Jesus Christ means being vulnerable to the fresh winds of the Holy Spirit and all the life changes this entails.

Philip Yancey recalls a story from Søren Kierkegaard about the peculiar mathematics in the kingdom of God:

> He [Kierkegaard] tells of a vandal who breaks into a department store at night and does not steal anything but rather rearranges all the price tags. The next day shopkeepers, not to mention the delighted customers, encounter such oddities as diamond necklaces on sale for a dollar and cheap costume-jewelry earrings costing thousands. The gospel is like that, says Kierkegaard: it changes around all our normal assumptions about worth and value.[4]

The fresh winds of the Holy Spirit shatter all our normal assumptions about worth and value, and the Christian life is a lifelong journey of discovering the *gospel's* assumptions about worth and value, and then opening our lives to the courageous new world to which these assumptions lead us. Like Ian, we learn that the gospel has the audacity to ask us to abandon our old vision of life and embrace a new vision born in the heart of God. And like those third-century Roman parents, we may even find ourselves stunned that the gospel places the peculiar demands of discipleship on literally everything about us, everything from friends and family relationships to entertainment, jobs, money, and sex.

The question of this chapter is, Once a person is forgiven, what next? Is there more to a relationship with God than knowing that the wrongs in my life are no longer held against me and that God has wiped the slate clean? This question brings us to a subject that theologians through the centuries have called *sanctification*. At the heart of the word *sanctify* is the blessing of God, the holiness of God, and the consecration of a person's life in the service of God. Sanctification is the work of the Holy Spirit who changes our lives in conformity with the mind of Christ, who plants within us God's vision of human life, and who empowers us to embody divine love in our own flesh and blood. One of the prayers after Holy Communion in the 1946 *Book of Common Worship* asks God to "so enrich us by the Holy Spirit that the life of Jesus may be made manifest in us, and the remainder of our days may be spent in Thy love and service."[5] This is the new life God gives: to have the love and sacrifice of Jesus made manifest in us every day and in every relationship. And this is the gift of the Holy Spirit: to have the remainder of our days spent in God's love and service.

If justification concerns the gift of a relationship with God, then sanctification addresses how we live and mature with the gift, and how the gift itself affects every aspect of our lives. Shirley Guthrie explains it this way:

> Justification tells us how a person becomes a Christian. Sanctification tells us how a person grows as a Christian.
> Justification tells us about God's gracious action toward us. Sanctification tells us about our response with obedient action toward God.
> Justification tells us that God is *for* us, forgiving and saving us from sin. Sanctification tells us that by the Holy Spirit the same God works *in* us, helping us to leave our sin behind and begin a new and radically different kind of life.
> In justification the covenant-making God makes a promise: "I will be your God." In sanctification, the same God also gives an inescapable command: "You shall be my people."
> Justification tells us that Christ is our Savior who died for us. Sanctification tells us that the same Christ is our Lord who commands us to live for him.[6]

Do you believe it is possible for people to change? The gospel answers with a whole-hearted *Yes*, because the gift of forgiveness means that we do not have to remain prisoners of our past mistakes and repeated failures; God gives new life. We are not, thanks be to God, merely the sum of all the broken parts of our lives; God gives new life. Indeed, "If anyone is in Christ, there is a new creation: everything old has passed away; see, everything has become new!" (2 Cor. 5:17).

One of the basic assumptions of the Bible is that God is the owner of everyone and everything. "The earth is the Lord's and all that is in it, the world, and those who live in it" (Ps. 24:1), sings the psalmist in jubilant praise. Would anything about your life change were you to become more sharply focused on God's ownership of every aspect of your life? Would your words to others be different? Would your relationships change at all? And what about your use of time and money? Would you be more or less focused on buying and consuming and accumulating? And how about your body: Would the way you treat it with food and alcohol and exercise be the same or different? How do your hormones and genitals figure into the equation? Would your sex life be different were you to acknowledge that even this most intimate aspect of your life is framed by God's ownership? Try an experiment. Take out your checkbook and review your typical use of money by looking at each expenditure through this filter: Is the will of God reflected in your use of money? And what story do your expenditures tell about your highest loyalties and deepest commitments? Questions such as these point us toward the very "stuff" of sanctification because they nourish in us the desire to grow in God's grace, even when painful changes are required. In *The Cost of Discipleship*, Dietrich Bonhoeffer, who was martyred by the Nazis during World War II, says it this way, *"Only he who believes is obedient, and only he who is obedient believes."* Obedience follows faith in the same way that good fruit grows on a tree.[7] How is the fruit of your life related to the faith you profess?

Self-Denial and the Costly
Grace of the Cross

These issues of obedience inevitably bring us to one of the foundational truths of the New Testament: In Jesus Christ, the old self dies and a new self is born. When Paul speaks of the new creation in Christ, he is not referring to a Pollyanna world chock-full of blissful daydreams and wishful thinking; he is speaking of nothing less than spiritual death and rebirth. Growing in grace is not a mere rearranging of the furniture but a wholesale starting over. In fact, the death of the old self and the birth of the new is one of the fundamental realities of baptism. As a person passes through the waters of baptism, we are given a symbol both of the washing away of sin *and* the death of the old self followed by the resurrection to new life. This may sound somewhat primitive to our modern ears, but few ideas are more central to the New Testament. In Ephesians, Paul addresses the demand of the gospel that we put away the practices of a pagan world:

> You were taught to put away your former way of life, your old self, corrupt and deluded by its lusts, and to be renewed in the spirit of your minds, and to clothe yourselves with the new self, created according to the likeness of God in true righteousness and holiness. (Eph. 4:22–24)

Then in the context of a moving passage on the power of the cross, Paul addresses the same point in his correspondence with the church at Rome. His critics are accusing him of giving open license to sin. If we are justified by grace, then what does it matter whether we sin or not? In fact, contend the critics, if God is simply going to forgive us anyway, then we might as well enjoy all the sin we can! As W. H. Auden has written, "Every crook will argue: 'I like committing crimes. God likes forgiving them. Really the world is admirably arranged.'"[8] So Paul answers his Roman critics with a word of costly grace:

> We know that our old self was crucified with him [Christ] so that the body of sin might be destroyed, and we might no longer be enslaved to sin. For whoever has died is free from sin. But if we have died with Christ, we believe that we will also live with him. (Rom. 6:6–8)

We find this theme also in Paul's letter to the Colossians, where he addresses the day-to-day impact of Christ's cross and resurrection in the lives of believers, declaring that our lives are "hidden with Christ in God":

> Do not lie to one another, seeing that you have stripped off the old self with its practices and have clothed yourselves with the new self, which is being renewed in knowledge according to the image of its creator. (Col. 3:9–10)

Why do you suppose that such passages are given short shrift in today's church? Could it be that they challenge us in ways that we don't like to be challenged? Yes, maybe these ideas lead us to the threshold of personal sacrifice in a culture that teaches us to accumulate all we can rather than give anything up. I happen to believe that we don't hear much about the death of the old self and the birth of the new self because at the heart of such language is the suggestion that we should actually divest ourselves of the things of this world that we have come to treasure more than God. We want the Christian faith, but we want it easy and on our terms. We crave the new creation promised by the gospel, but we want it without the death of the old self. But this simply cannot be had; it would like having Easter without Good Friday.

So we live in a church where all ideologies and lifestyles are lauded under the broad canopy of inclusiveness, but no one wants to surrender anything. We want the promises of the gospel without the challenge, the succor of knowing we belong to Christ without any of his requirements for a faithful life. We cherish the words of forgiveness but spurn the fruits of forgiveness in our lives. And the prophet Elijah asks us today, just as he did the Israelites of old, "How long will you go limping with two different opinions?" (1 Kgs. 18:21). As Bonhoeffer once wrote,

> Cheap grace is the deadly enemy of our Church. We are fighting today for costly grace. . . .
> Cheap grace is the preaching of forgiveness without requiring repentance, baptism without church discipline, Communion without confession, absolution without personal confession. Cheap grace is grace without discipleship, grace without the cross, grace without Jesus Christ, living and incarnate.
> Costly grace is the treasure hidden in the field; for the sake of it a man will gladly go and sell all that he has. It is the pearl of great price to buy which the merchant will sell all his goods. . . . Costly grace is the gospel which must be *sought* again and again, the gift which must be *asked* for, the door at which a man must *knock*.[9]

Growing in grace means the abandonment of cheap grace and the total surrender of one's life to Jesus Christ. C. S. Lewis has said it this way:

> Christ says "Give me All. I don't want so much of your time and so much of your money and so much of your work: I want You. I have not come to torment your natural self, but to kill it. No half-measures are any good. I don't want to cut off a branch here and a branch there, I want to have the whole tree down. I don't want to drill the tooth, or crown it, or stop it, but to have it out. Hand over the whole natural self. . . . I will give you a new self instead. In fact, I will give you Myself: my own will shall become yours."[10]

We are called to surrender our all to God, because Christian grace is grace *with* discipleship, grace *with* the cross, grace *with* Jesus Christ, living and incarnate.

We can soften it all we want, and we can dodge it from here to kingdom come, but all who want to be disciples of Jesus Christ must finally face the inescapable summons of our Lord:

> If any want to become my followers, let them deny themselves and take up their cross and follow me. For those who want to save their life will lose it, and those who lose their life for my sake, and for the sake of the gospel, will

save it. For what will it profit them to gain the whole world and forfeit their life? (Mark 8:34b–37)

We might as well confront it head-on. In the Christian faith, salvation is more than a cozy little deal we cut with God that allows us to snuggle up in divine comfort and let the world go blithely by, and neither is it a one-way ticket to health, wealth, and success. The forgiveness of sins is a beginning, not an end, and one of the major problems the church faces today is getting that through our thick skulls. Somehow we got the idea along the way that "getting saved" is mainly about the state of our souls, *but nothing, absolutely nothing could be more patently untrue.* Once again, the Westminster Shorter Catechism begins by saying that the chief end of human life is to glorify God and to enjoy God forever.[11] The entire Christian life is framed inside that conviction. John Leith has observed,

> The glory of God and his purposes in the world are more important than the salvation of one's own soul. Personal salvation can be a very selfish act. Berdyaev paints a horrible picture of those who trample over their neighbors in the crush to get through the gates of heaven. Those Calvinists who asked candidates for the ministry if they were willing to be damned for the glory of God were trying to root out the last element of self-seeking in religion. Human beings are religious, the Calvinist asserts, not to justify their needs or to give meaning to their lives but because God has created them and called them to his service.[12]

This word is often silenced today by the cacophony of voices clamoring for self-affirmation. Strangely, the psychological language of self-esteem and self-worth have replaced the Bible's unequivocal emphasis on self-denial, personal sacrifice, and the surrender of the self for the sake of a higher good. I remember once, years ago, feeling that the children's sermon in the Sunday service had become entirely too cutesy and too much like "show-time." The little ones, in my view, were being exploited for the entertainment of their parents and were being taught the inappropriate lesson that, if only for a few minutes, they were the center of worship. So I suggested that we change the custom of having the children sit on the chancel steps (where they could look out and perform for an adoring public) and ask them instead to sit in the first two pews facing the chancel like everyone else. That way they would not be on display, and I hoped to have a better chance at holding their attention. My proposal was met with mixed reactions, but I shall never forget that one of the adult responses was, "There they go, pushing the children aside!" I was stunned by the revelation that not only were some of the parents completely comfortable with the "show and tell" genre of children's sermons but that was exactly what some of them wanted in the church's cafeteria of goods and services. They wanted their children to experience themselves as the center of worship for that one, brief, shining moment. Somehow this was gratifying for the parents (I don't think the children cared where they sat), making them feel better about themselves and the caring ethos of their church.

As picayune as that situation may seem in the broader context of the church's life, in my mind it is emblematic of the ego-driven culture that has made for itself a nice cushy nest inside the church and of the ego-driven appetite to which we expect the church to cater. The language of self-denial speaks to people like an unintelligible voice from an alien planet in an unknown galaxy. One thing is certain: it is all but incomprehensible in a culture incessantly preoccupied with how people feel about things in general, how their religion makes them feel about themselves, and how they feel about how they feel. As Cornelius Plantinga Jr. points out, "In an ego-centered culture, wants become needs (maybe even duties), the self replaces the soul, and human life degenerates into the clamor of competing autobiographies. . . . In such a culture, . . . the self exists to be explored, indulged, and expressed but not disciplined or restrained."[13] The doctrine of sanctification, however, is precisely about such discipline and restraint; apart from it, it is impossible to experience the new life God gives us in Jesus Christ.

In a Christian context, self-denial never means self-hatred or self-loathing, nor does it involve looking in the mirror every morning to a chorus of voices inside your head all chanting in unison, "What a worm am I!" Neither does self-denial mean thinking of yourself as a human doormat and allowing others to walk all over you. A healthy respect for oneself as a human being created in the image of God, as well as loved and redeemed by God, is a foundational part of the Christian's self-understanding. Reflecting on the God-given dignity of human life, the psalmist asks God, "[W]hat are human beings that you are mindful of them, mortals that you care for them?" (8:4). Self-denial is not about person bashing; it is about setting aside every desire and want and hunger that keep us from loving God with all our heart and soul and mind and strength, and our neighbor as ourselves. It recognizes with unflinching honesty that we humans suffer from what Calvin calls "swollen souls":[14]

> But there is no one who does not cherish within himself some opinion of his own pre-eminence. Thus each individual, by flattering himself, bears a kind of kingdom in his breast.[15]

Self-denial involves the painful but certain acknowledgment that our devotion to self is often so totally blown out of all proportion to every other devotion in our lives that it corrupts the love of God and neighbor. This is why the gospel calls us to exclude everything in our lives that stands in the way of following Jesus Christ exclusively. In the words of Bonhoeffer: "When we are called to follow Christ, we are summoned to an exclusive attachment to his person."[16]

> The cross is laid on every Christian. The first Christ-suffering which every man must experience is the call to abandon the attachments of this world. It is the dying of the old man which is the result of his encounter with Christ. As we embark upon discipleship we surrender ourselves to Christ in union with his death—we give over our lives to death. Thus it begins; the cross is not the terrible end to an otherwise godfearing and happy life, but it meets us at the beginning of our communion with Christ. When Christ calls a man, he bids him come and die. It may be a death like that of the first disciples who had to leave home and work to follow him, or it may be a death like Luther's, who had to leave the monastery and go out into the world. But it is the same death every time—death in Jesus Christ, the death of the old man at his call. . . .[17]

A scene in Alan Paton's novel *Ah, But Your Land Is Beautiful* paints a moving portrait of self-denial. Robert Mansfield is a white South African headmaster, who one day resigns his post because his school is not permitted to compete against a team from a black school in a sporting event. Mansfield thinks the decision is patently wrong, and he comes to the painful realization that he cannot preside over an institution that would permit such bigoted injustice. Facing his responsibilities as a Christian, Mansfield resigns.

After the resignation, a black man named Emmanuel Nene pays Mansfield a visit, saying that he came to meet the man of courage who had resigned his livelihood because of his convictions, and he wants to shake the hand of the man whose daily life was molded by such a living faith. In the conversation, however, Nene lets it be known that he has also come for another reason. He wants Mansfield to know that he has decided to join a multiracial political party and join the fight for racial equality. He knows this will brand him as a radical and make him an enemy of the state, but this is what he has resolved to do. Mansfield warns Nene of some of the consequences he will surely suffer. "Yes, I understand," says Nene. "I know I am going to get wounded not only by the government but by my own people as well, just like you." Then as Nene stands and prepares to leave, he turns to Mansfield with these words: "You know, I don't worry about the wounds. When I go up there, which is my intention, the big Judge will say, 'Where are your wounds? Wasn't there anything worth fighting for? And I just couldn't face that question.' "[18]

Where are your wounds? Where is the evidence of self-denial in your life? The choices of Robert Mansfield and Emmanuel Nene suggest the selfless sacrifice at the heart of the Christian life. After forgiveness, what next? The gospel is clear: sacrificial choices, self-giving love, barriers that divide neighbors torn down, time-honored prejudices extinguished. And the stabbing question: Where are your wounds?

Faith Working through Love

What, then, is involved in learning the way of self-denial? As I have already suggested, the gift of faith leaves no aspect of life untouched. It affects our behavior in the living room as well as the bedroom; in the boardroom as well as the dining room. And faith touches the whole range of human emotions and longings and desires and motives. In the fifth chapter of Galatians, Paul suggests that, as we embrace the gift of faith in all the realities of everyday life, "the only thing that counts is faith working through love" (5:6b). Paul continues:

> For you were called to freedom, brothers and sisters; only do not use your freedom as an opportunity for self-indulgence, but through love become slaves to one another. For the whole law is summed up in a single commandment, "You shall love your neighbor as yourself." (Gal. 5:13–14)

If faith is genuine, it will manifest itself in love. If faith is real, if faith is more than empty words recited by rote, it will not be content to sit idly by but will become active in words and deeds of self-giving love. To be sure, Christian love is not to be confused with the cheap sentimentality we typically see in the popular novel or movie or TV sitcom. And it has absolutely nothing to do with befriending another person so long as we're getting something in return, a handy little "You scratch my back and I'll scratch yours" arrangement. Much to the contrary, *the love of the gospel is love that is gladly willing to make personal sacrifice for the sake of the beloved.* It is love that is willing to look at all the raw implications of being in relationship with others and, as Paul describes it, remain patient and kind, not envious or boastful or arrogant or rude, not insistent on its own way, not irritable or resentful. This is the love of God that never rejoices in wrongdoing, but only rejoices in the truth—the love that "bears all things, believes all things, hopes all things, endures all things" (1 Cor. 13:4–7). The love we receive through God's forgiveness is never content to be hoarded as a private possession but is always restless to be spent. As Barth says, "And faith itself would not be faith if it did not work by love, if it were not as Luther put it 'a living, active, busy thing.'"[19]

One of the main ways in which faith becomes a living, active, busy thing is in the realm of personal relationships, as sins are forgiven and bridges of reconciliation built. This, of course, is perhaps the hardest message of the gospel to internalize and act on, because it brings us to the deep hurt that others have inflicted on us, as well as feelings of animosity that are difficult to shake. But Jesus taught his followers in the face of strained relationships and hurt feelings to pray, "Forgive us our debts, *as we also have forgiven our debtors*" (Matt. 6:12, emphasis added), and one would be hard-pressed to find a more urgent need in the strife-ridden contention of today's world.

Sweet revenge . . . Whether it's warring factions squaring off in the Middle East or two individuals facing an embittered past, I would venture to say that the deepest and bloodiest wounds in the human heart grow out of the need both to give and to receive forgiveness. Sometimes forgiveness is hard to receive because it's difficult to admit a wrong and to be humble enough to be on the receiving end of another person's grace. Yet forgiveness is often incredibly hard to give, isn't it? A spouse did the unthinkable. A child brought unbearable strife into the home. A coworker left you high and dry, just when you really needed someone to stand by you. A neighbor insulted you with a damaging piece of gossip. A brother or sister committed a treason that threatens to sever the ties that bind. And how do we respond? We fume. We stew. We hurt. We sulk. We grieve. We harbor resentment. We hold a grudge. Sometimes we retaliate. And in and through it all, the hurt continues and the wound gets deeper. But the gospel of Jesus Christ calls us to forgiveness, not resentment; to reconciliation, not animosity. What we often forget is that forgiveness, like the very grace of God, is never a matter of what people deserve but of the totally unmerited, gracious love of God given to the *un*deserving and *un*worthy and *un*lovable. Do I deserve the grace of God? Indeed not. Am I worthy of the love of Jesus Christ? Without a doubt, no. No one is worthy of the forgiveness of the cross, but if God were to wait until we deserve it, we would never receive divine forgiveness and would be doomed to the endless treadmill of past mistakes and failures. But the good news is that God has entirely blotted out our mistakes and failures with the promise "I love you anyway!" And once we have received God's marvelous forgiveness, our job in life is to give it away, to spend it liberally, to share it lavishly even with those who have hurt us. So we pray, Forgive us our sins, O God, just as we are willing to forgive those who have injured us, mocked us, offended us, taken us for granted, and used us. Forgive us, Lord, and protect us from every desire to keep your forgiveness just for ourselves.

In 1983, *Time* magazine carried a photo that flashed across the world. It was a picture of Pope John Paul II and Mehmet Ali Agca, the would-be assassin who tried to murder the Pope. The story that accompanied the photo said, in part,

Last week, in an extraordinary moment of grace, the violence in St. Peter's Square was transformed. In a bare white-walled cell in Rome's Rebibbia prison, John Paul tenderly held the hand that held the gun that was meant to kill him. For 21 minutes, the Pope sat with his would-be assassin, Mehmet Ali Agca. The two talked softly. Once or twice Agca laughed. The Pope forgave him for the shooting. At the end of the meeting, Agca either kissed the Pope's ring or pressed the Pope's hand to his forehead in a Muslim gesture of respect.[20]

This, I suggest, is a living picture of "faith working through love": The victim and the perpetrator are reconciled through the mercy of the victim.

Lazarus and Discipleship: Learning the Way of the Cross in the Midst of Affluence

Money, sex, politics, power . . . These, it seems, are the themes that, on any given day, make the world go 'round, and part of the process of growing in the grace of God is learning the way of the gospel in a culture where competing ideologies and loyalties constantly pull and tug at us. While this is a subject that makes many of us squirm in our pew, one of the most pressing issues facing American Christians today is the responsible stewardship of money. In fact, some of the most fertile ground for exploring the meaning of sanctification is learning to live as authentic disciples of Jesus Christ in the affluent niche of the American pie so familiar to most Presbyterians. For the purpose of illustration, I invite you to turn to Luke 16:19–31 where we find the parable of the Rich Man and Lazarus.

Picture it as a drama in three acts. The curtain has just gone up on the first act to reveal center stage an individual who lives a life of untold wealth. He dresses to the nines and feasts sumptuously every day; his is a life not just of privilege but of ostentatious luxury. But while he lives the life of royalty, at the gate of his grand estate is a poor man named Lazarus who is so desperately impoverished that his only food comes in the form of scraps from the rich man's table. There he is, day by day, in full view of the rich man. And there he suffers, covered with sores and aching for compassion. In the course of time, both Lazarus and the rich man die. End of Act I.

Act II—curtain up. In death, Lazarus has ascended to the bosom of Abraham, while the rich man finds himself in Hades, living a life of incessant torment. The rich man appeals to his kinship with Father Abraham, but Abraham reminds him, "In your lifetime, you received many good things and, in like manner, Lazarus received evil things. Now your fortunes are reversed, and there is nothing to be done about it because, as you can see, a great chasm has been fixed between you and us. The way you lived your life on earth was a foreshadowing of your destiny. In fact, every step is destiny. The choices you make are destiny." End of Act II.

As the curtain goes up on Act III, the rich man offers an impassioned plea for Abraham to send Lazarus back from the dead to warn the rich man's five brothers so that they won't make the same choices and find themselves eventually in the same torment. But Abraham refuses. "They have already been warned by God," he says. "They have Moses and the prophets, and they know what scripture teaches—to do justice, to love kindness, and to walk humbly with their God. If they refuse to listen to the testimony of God's Word, then neither will they be convinced by the miracle of someone rising from the dead." End of play.

Pretty stout words for growing in grace, aren't they? To start with, read in the context of the whole of scripture, this parable does *not* negate everything we have already said about salvation as a gift of God's grace rather than good works. Jesus does, however, declare in a rather pointed way that the substance of our lives reveals whether our faith is real, deep, and enduring, or whether it amounts to hollow ritual that actually means very little when we do things like go to the bank and sit down at table with friends and buy our cars and go to the country club and give to the church and decorate our homes and order all our priorities in life. Indeed, good works do not earn us salvation; they are the *fruit* of salvation. But if the fruit is missing, the authenticity of faith is in question. Is the faith we profess a truth or a lie? "So let our lips *and lives* express the holy gospel we profess,"[21] Isaac Watts suggests. And as Luther once said, "Good works do not make a good [person], but a good [person] does good works."[22]

Lazarus is at the door, our Lord tells us. And the Lazarus at our door is suffering. He is hungry, homeless, and hopeless. Lazarus is the little child who goes to bed hungry while children across town fill their stomachs with every good food imaginable. Lazarus is the third-world baby who has been born to poverty and doesn't stand a chance in life. Lazarus is the woman parked on the doorstep of a shelter where women show up battered and bruised 365 days of the year. Lazarus is the person who once owned a home and had a modest income but for whom one day the bottom fell out, his luck dried up, and the bank foreclosed on his house. Now he moves from one relative to another and shuffles from one agency to another, in order to survive by one hand-out after another. It's a humiliating existence. He hears that the American economy is thriving and that people are getting rich, but all he gets is poorer. Lazarus also is the person who doesn't even have relatives to bounce between, who doesn't have a place to shower and get cleaned up for a job interview and who shows up for the interview stinking to high heaven because there is no money for the laundromat. Lazarus is also the single mother with no income to feed her children. Most days, she feels sad and hopeless because the people who are in a position to help her merely look down their noses at her. And Lazarus is the person dying of AIDS who has become an expendable castoff of society, neatly disposed of by his "friends" because his sexuality has become a social embarrassment.

These are the Lazaruses who lie prostrate at the gates of our cities and neighborhoods, and these are the needs that affluent Americans have conditioned themselves not to see because reaching out in any significant way would be far too costly. It would mean a change of attitude concerning the aches and cries of the wounded. It would mean reexamining those structures and systems of society that are callous to injustice. It would mean trying to put ourselves in the shoes of a person with AIDS who is shunned and isolated. It would mean identifying with a little child with a swollen belly across the world. And it would cut into the luxuries that we have fooled ourselves into thinking are necessities. Make no mistake, the parable of the Rich Man and Lazarus is not only about money, but it *is* about money. It's about the willingness or unwillingness of those who travel the affluent corridors of American society to spend their resources on the outrageous needs of the Lazaruses of this world who lie in suffering and want while the more fortunate go merrily on an extended shopping spree. The gospel tells us plainly that we are all directly accountable to God for how we use our material possessions, and one of the gravest of all dangers for disciples of Jesus Christ is allowing the privileges of wealth to insulate us from the raw, aching cries of human need all around us. But beyond the thorny issue of money, the parable of the Rich Man and Lazarus presses the question of basic human attitudes: Will our lives be turned inward on our selves or outward to the needs of human pain? "The Lazaruses of the world deserve it!" is the denouncement often heard. "They need to get a job and do an honest day's work! I've worked hard for my money, and if I want to spend it on the luxuries I've earned, that's my right!" But do we not hear in all of this the voice of love? "Through love become slaves of one another. For the whole law is summed up in a single commandment. 'You shall love your neighbor as yourself'" (Gal. 5:13b–14).

Archbishop Desmond Tutu asks us to think of the poor man by the gate of Lazarus's mansion as a brother in our own family. Assume, for a moment, that a member of your own family is in dire trouble. You would do everything in your power to help that family member, wouldn't you? You would even be willing to make sacrifices because you want the very best for your family. We all want the very best for those we truly love. We want good education and health care and are willing to do everything in our power, even to the point of sacrifice, to make it happen. If members of our family were victimized and oppressed, would we not move heaven and earth to speak out against that victimization and oppression? If members of our family were having their human rights violated by ruthless dictators, would we stand idly by, fold our hands in our lap, bow our heads for prayer, and conclude, "Oh, that's not my business"? Of course not, because where family is concerned, we want the best.[23] And growing in God's grace involves waking up to the fact that we are not the only people on the planet and that, in Jesus Christ, all of God's children are our brothers and sisters.

I have been unable to find the origin of this statement, but someone has rightly observed that the Christian life begins with "a holy discontent" with things as they are. In other words, the world is not as God wants it to be, and our job as disciples of the risen Christ is to work for the world God wants. Such is the substance of "faith working through love."

Sanctification: The Sacrifice of Gratitude

Why would anyone willingly choose such a life? How remarkably out of step it sounds! How absurd! What utter nonsense! In this power-mongering world, the strong survive and the weak are losers; everybody with half a brain knows that. And the convictions at the heart of "a holy discontent" are never the passions that drive the stock market to higher summits or the bottom line of the ledger to an ever-larger margin of profit or the network of social relations at the country club. But they are precisely the passions that lay the foundation for a life in which faith is active in love, a life that has surrendered gladly and willingly and joyously and totally to the lordship of Jesus Christ, even if it means abandoning old ways of life and embracing an invisible kingdom in which all assumptions of value and worth are turned upside down and inside out. And consider this: *These passions form the human face of gratitude in response to God's gracious love. We choose to live this way because we are thankful for a love undeserved. We are grateful for a mercy that was given to us despite our worst selves.*

Gratitude, finally, is the heart of sanctification. The life that is growing in grace is a life driven by gratitude to the God who so loved the world that Jesus Christ died on the cross and rose from the grave. Martin Luther offers this moving account of his personal gratitude before God:

> Well now! My God has given to me, unworthy and lost man, without any merit, absolutely for nothing and out of pure mercy, through and in Christ, the full riches of all godliness and blessedness, so that I henceforth need nothing more than to believe it is so.

Well, then, for such a Father, who has so prodigally lavished upon me his blessings, I will in return freely, joyously and for nothing do what is well-pleasing to Him, and also be a Christian toward my neighbor, as Christ has been to me; and I will do nothing except only what I see to be needful, useful and blessed for him, because I indeed throughout my faith have enough of everything in Christ. See, thus there flows from faith love and delight in God, and from love a free, willing, joyous life to serve our neighbor for nothing. For just as our neighbor suffers want and is in need of our superabundance, so have we suffered want before God and been in need of his grace.

Therefore, as God through Christ has helped us for nothing, so ought we through the body and its works to do nothing but help our neighbor.[24]

What are the marks of gratitude in your own life? And what is the evidence that you personally are growing in grace?

Truth 6

God Is Revealed in the Bible

Your word is a lamp to my feet and a light to my path.

(Ps. 119:105)

The Thorny Question of Authority

These reflections on our life together began with the whole story of salvation recorded in the Bible, and the succeeding chapters have highlighted some of the main themes of the story. In the next chapter, we will turn our thoughts to the nature and character of the church as the body of Christ. But first, what is the role of the Bible as a book in the church's life? What do Presbyterians believe about the canon of scripture?

The hotbed of controversy in today's church is fueled, in large measure, by the myriad social issues that litter the landscape of American culture. In the overall milieu of these controversies, one major issue rocking the church is the nature and authority of the Bible. It may not always be debated as such, but all the hot issues that threaten to drive us straight into the arms of schism are rooted in the authority of scripture both in the life of the individual believer and in the life of the community of faith. Are we to interpret the Bible literally or figuratively? And how is a person to figure out which reading to apply to which passages? Should such disciplines as science and history and anthropology inform our reading of scripture? If so, how much weight do they carry in shaping our interpretation? And to what extent should the books of the Bible be read as products of the customs and mores of the various cultures in which they arose? Name an issue, any issue, and I would venture to say that lurking behind and beneath the rancor of dispute is the broader issue of how to interpret the Bible and what authority the Bible holds in the life of faith.

One of the hallmarks of the Reformation was an extremely high view of scripture. Martin Luther and John Calvin both understood that the crying need which they faced was restoring the sixteenth-century church to its biblical roots, and their insistence on doing so was rooted nowhere but in the Bible itself. The psalmist describes the Word of God as a divine lamp illumining the path we tread through all the uncertainties of life. Throughout the Old Testament, the covenant community is constantly admonished to pass the faith from generation to generation by telling the sacred story of salvation. In the New Testament, 2 Timothy makes the audacious claim that "all scripture is inspired by God and is useful for teaching, for reproof, for correction, and for training in righteousness, so that everyone who belongs to God may be proficient, equipped for every good work" (3:16–17). One of the problems we face today, however, is that modern Christians are not much interested in reproof and correction, not to mention the miracle of God's life-changing Word. After all, any standard that would be used to reprove and correct is a moving target because we all get to determine and define our own standard. Our culture has taught us that we are endowed with this inalienable right, this sacred privilege, and the presumption to end all presumption is that of imposing a standard of belief and conduct on anyone else. And one of the most remarkable things is that this view is as common as the air we breathe not only outside the church in secular culture but inside the church where we have presumably submitted ourselves first to Jesus Christ as Lord and Head and second to our brothers and sisters in Christ.

Do you understand that the voice of the living God speaks to you personally through the words of the Bible? Does it occupy a place in your life alongside other respected books, or does the Bible possess an authority unlike all other books, all other sources of revelation? And what about your congregation? In the sermons you hear and the various discussions that take place around the church, is God's Word used merely as a prop first for one opinion and then another, or does your congregation turn to the Bible as the living source of God's self-revelation that draws us into relationship with Jesus Christ?

Each time a deacon, elder, or minister in the Presbyterian Church is ordained to office, he or she must say, "Yes" to the following question: "Do you accept the Scriptures of the Old and New Testaments to be, by the Holy Spirit, the unique and authoritative witness to Jesus Christ in the Church universal, and God's Word to you?"[1] Indeed, what do "unique" and "authoritative" mean in a world where all claims to truth are relative and the final authority is the self? The Confession of 1967 goes so far as to say that "the Scriptures are not a witness among others, but the witness without parallel."[2] In an earlier era, the Larger Catechism described the Bible by saying that "the holy Scriptures of the Old and New Testaments are the Word of God, the only rule of faith and obedience," and then proceeded to affirm the principal message of the Bible: to teach what we are to believe concerning God and what duty God requires of us.[3]

These claims are indeed bold and daring, even courageous, in such a world as ours. Entrenched as we are in the American soil of unbridled individualism, each individual is her or his own authority in all aspects of life. And, as for religion, well, religion is very personal, so everybody should just leave me alone while *I* decide what *I* believe. In *Habits of the Heart*, Robert Bellah writes of a woman named Sheila, who says,

> I believe in God. I'm not a religious fanatic. I can't remember the last time I went to church. My faith has carried me a long way. It's Sheilaism. Just my own little voice.[4]

The folks in our pews and Sunday school classes may be different from Sheila in that they come to church more often, but I guarantee you that they bring many of Sheila's cultural assumptions with them and they view their work, their family, the world in general, and even the church in extremely individualistic terms. Yes, just my own little voice, that's all I need—Sheilaism. Eugene Peterson tells the story of "a life-long reader of the Bible, who one day realized that his life wasn't turning out as he thought the Bible promised that it would; he decided then and there to 'make my life my authority instead of the Bible.' "[5]

But faithfulness to Jesus Christ is never rooted in the paltry claims of my tiny life in one minuscule corner of the world. Rather, issues of personal discipleship are the subject of my lifelong encounter with Jesus Christ in and through scripture. Following him can never be divorced from the experience of being called and forgiven and changed by Jesus Christ through the story of the Bible. Peterson continues,

> We do not form our personal spiritual lives from a random assemblage of favorite texts in combination with individual circumstances; we are formed by the Holy Spirit following the text of Holy Scriptures. God does not put us in charge of forming our personal spiritualities. We grow in accordance with the revealed Word implanted in us by the Spirit.[6]

As uncomfortable as this may make us, the claims of the Reformed tradition fly directly in the face of a church in which "the way, the truth, and the life" (John 14:6) is often supplanted by the shifting sand of *my* truth, *your* truth, *her* truth, *his* truth, *anybody's* truth, and *everybody's* truth.

The time is indeed ripe to open ourselves anew to the spirit of the Reformation and return to our biblical roots. The renewal of the church will not happen in our day unless and until we face up to *the* issue beneath all of our issues. As we do so, what can we learn about the nature and authority of the Bible from the faithful who have gone before us? What do the blood of the martyrs and the faith of the ages teach us about the place of holy scripture in the believer's life? Let me venture a few central claims:

1. The Bible is indeed the written Word of God and, therefore, the means of God's self-revelation.
2. The Bible reveals, by the power of the Holy Spirit, Jesus Christ who is himself the living and eternal Word of God (cf. John 1:1ff).
3. The Bible rests on the authority of God and authoritatively speaks God's Word to believers in all times and places, in all cultures and contexts.
4. The Bible is unique, unlike all other books and all other claims to divine revelation.
5. The Bible is God's Word both to the church as a body and to each of us as individuals.
6. Everything we need to know for faith and obedience is contained in the scriptures of the Old and New Testaments.
7. By the power of the Holy Spirit, the Word of God can re-create even the contentious, strife-driven church of today.[7]

These claims may seem a bit audacious, even presumptuous, and perhaps out of step with these modern times. Yet they are at the heart of what Presbyterians believe as "people of the Book." The scriptures of the Old and New Testaments are nothing other than the very basis of our life together as the body of Jesus Christ. In the words of Karl Barth,

> Where the Church is alive, it will always be having to re-assess itself by this standard. We must always be putting the question, 'What is the evidence?' Not the evidence of my thoughts, or my heart, but the evidence of the apostles and prophets, as the evidence of God's self-evidence.[8]

Scripture As Divine Revelation

This brings us to the conviction that God has chosen to reveal himself through the Bible. My hunch is that, in today's culture, the phrase "divine revelation" is one of those distinguished-sounding, textbookish terms that instantaneously produces glassy eyes and distant stares. Let me suggest, however, that divine revelation raises one of the most fundamental questions of all, one that has repeatedly guided us in the preceding chapters: As we contemplate the faithfulness to which God calls us, *what is our starting point*? Do our beliefs begin with God or with human experience? Said another way, Do we begin with God and understand ourselves as a result of God's self-revelation in Jesus Christ, or do we begin with ourselves and gradually come to know God as a byproduct of our self-understanding? While, at first glance, this may seem to tilt the discussion in a decidedly academic or theoretical direction, I assure you that this is an immensely practical question with enormous ramifications that are difficult to overstate. A mixed response to this question has created a fog of confusion enveloping today's church, not to mention the glut of special-interest agendas, each of which offers a starting point specifically tailored to serve predetermined ends. In answering the question "Where do we start?" our beliefs are already given an initial posture and shape that will affect every later conclusion. What, after all, is the foundation on which we endeavor to build our lives before God? John Calvin insists that we begin not with ourselves, but with God: "Again, it is certain that man never achieves a clear knowledge of himself unless he has first looked upon God's face, and then descends from contemplating him to scrutinize himself."[9]

Our source for contemplating God is scripture, because *it is scripture that reveals who God is*. As I suggested in our discussion of God's sovereignty, we know God only as God chooses to be revealed, and the self-revelation of God is the very heartbeat of scripture. The Bible is not a handy little list of "do's" and "don'ts" or a composite of divine suggestions garnered from the wisdom of the ages. Neither is it a utilitarian handbook of religious topics for use in the throes of theological debate. All too often, the Bible has been regarded as such, and the unfortunate result has been the abuse of scripture as a hammer to bludgeon one's opponents. But scripture will not be reduced to a collection of recipes for personal success or theological prowess. The Bible is the vessel God has chosen to convey the saving grace of Jesus Christ and to draw us into a relationship with him. Inspired by God, it is thoroughly *God's* Word, *God's* story, *God's* sovereign claim on human life. It tells us who God is and what God expects from us in our journeys through life. Affirming the Bible as divine revelation reminds us that "the great fact is God," and that grappling with the reality of God is the only authentic beginning of faithfulness. Furthermore, attempting to reach so-called Christian answers to the great questions of life apart from the Bible is bogus.

The Bible, though, is also a very human book, and unabashedly so. To be sure, it was born in the heart of God and is the voice of God to every time and place, to all cultures and societies, yet the Bible comes, just as surely, from the blood, sweat, and tears of the community of God's people across the ages. The Bible rises up out of the tear-stained agonies of Hebrew slaves in captivity; from the muddy banks of the Red Sea as the slaves were finally set free; from the incessant vulnerabilities of God's people as they grappled with the demands of obedience in the encircling pluralism of their age; and from the shackles and despair of exile. To say that the Bible is divinely inspired does not diminish its humanity one iota, for the words of scripture spring from the very soil of our humanness—warts, blemishes, and all. They grow from the humble submission of a young peasant girl named Mary who bore the Son of God into the world, and from the deadly stench of a bloody Friday when Mary's son was lynched by an evil mob. They come to life in the open wounds of Saint Paul as he suffered shipwreck, imprisonment, and beating for the sake of Jesus Christ, and from the blood of Christian martyrs across the generations. God inspired the writing of holy scripture, but not in a vacuum. The inspiration came through the clay feet of men, women, and children through the ages who were commandeered for the service of God.

Word and Spirit

One of the dangers of such a high view of scripture is that the Bible itself may become an object of worship and, thereby, a form of idolatry. Have you ever been in a theological conversation and had the sneaking suspicion that certain biblical texts were more important to some of the folks in the discussion than loving God and neighbor, or that they were chiefly interested not in hearing God speak but in winning their argument by wielding one or two passages from the Bible? Those who have hung around the church with much regularity, no doubt, have had that kind of experience and maybe even, in the heat of debate, have been guilty of it themselves. It is, therefore, imperative that we turn now to the power of the Holy Spirit to bring the Word of God to life in our hearts.

The words printed on the pages of the Bible are not, in and of themselves, the Word of God. Rather, they *become* the Word of God by the inward testimony of the Holy Spirit,[10] which is nothing less than a miracle. We do not worship the words printed on the page; we worship the God who is revealed *by the power of the Holy Spirit* through the words on the page. The Westminster Confession of Faith says it this way:

> Our full persuasion and assurance of the infallible truth and divine authority thereof, is from the inward work of the Holy Spirit, bearing witness by and with the Word in our hearts. The whole counsel of God, concerning all things necessary for his own glory, man's salvation, faith, and life, is either expressly set down in scripture, or by good and necessary consequence may

be deduced from Scripture. . . . Nevertheless we acknowledge the inward
illumination of the Spirit of God to be necessary for the saving understanding of such things as are revealed in the Word.[11]

It is likewise helpful to note that, in the Confession of 1967, the discussion of
the Bible occurs under the section entitled, "The Communion of the Holy
Spirit."[12] To speak of the Word of God without simultaneously speaking of the
power of the Holy Spirit is to sever the Word from its very source, because
the power to communicate and confirm the Word of God in our hearts rests
solely in the Holy Spirit.

In part, this view protects us from the idolatry of worshiping the Bible
rather than the God of the Bible, and it prevents us from enshrining texts
rather than revering the living Word. Yet this view reminds us that we are
completely dependent on the Holy Spirit in all matters pertaining to hearing
the Word of God and interpreting it for the times in which we live. It is entirely
beyond my power to convince anyone that John 3:16, for example, is the
Word of God simply because I say so and because I can point to the actual
words of John 3:16 printed on a page in the Bible. The authority to convince
and persuade is the authority of the Holy Spirit, and this is why the reading of
scripture and the preaching of the Word in Reformed worship is preceded by
the prayer that God will illumine our hearts and minds by the power of the
Holy Spirit. So we pray,

God our helper, show us your ways and teach us your paths. By your Holy
Spirit, open our minds that we may be led in your truth and taught your will.
Then may we praise you by listening to your Word and by obeying it;
through Jesus Christ our Lord. Amen.[13]

Jesus Christ, the Living Word

The conviction that the Holy Spirit is the source and vessel of the Word of
God leads us directly to Jesus Christ, the living Word. While the Bible is the
Word of God written, we interpret it specifically "in the light of its witness to
God's work of reconciliation in Christ."[14] If God's Word is nothing less than
God's self-revelation and, if God has supremely been revealed in the birth,
life, death, and resurrection of Jesus Christ, then our interpretation of scripture begins and ends with him. Jesus Christ is the lens through whom we see
God and come to know who God is, and all of scripture is to be interpreted in
light of what we know of God in Jesus Christ. Karl Barth has understood the
scriptures as "the document of the manifestation of the Word of God in the
person of Jesus Christ."[15] The Bible, the *written* Word of God, reveals Jesus

Christ, the *living* Word of God. It is Jesus Christ of whom John writes when he says, "In the beginning was the Word, and the Word was with God, and the Word was God" (John 1:1). In a similar vein, Paul affirms that Jesus Christ is "the image of the invisible God" (Col. 1:15a), suggesting that the person and work of Jesus Christ are like a prism refracting the light of God into our lives, by the power of the Holy Spirit. Jesus Christ himself gives meaning and content to what we read in the Bible. In fact, it is the purpose and will of Jesus Christ to which all of scripture bears witness, because Jesus Christ is himself the heart, the soul, and the substance of the Word of God. As the Theological Declaration of Barmen declares, "Jesus Christ, as he is attested for us in Holy Scripture, is the one Word of God which we have to hear and which we have to trust and obey in life and in death."[16]

Reading Scripture in Community:
Learning to Ask the Right Questions

We come now to a critical juncture: the practical matter of interpreting the Bible for the times in which we live. If everything we need to know for faithfulness to Jesus Christ can be found in the Bible, then why is there so much ugliness and party spirit at work in the church? While I certainly do not presume to offer you in these pages the be-all and end-all of Bible study, what I do offer you is a word of hope rooted in the grace of God. As in the rest of this book, there is nothing new here. This is an old, old word based on the simple premise that, in Jesus Christ, God continues to speak, and if anyone wants to hear that Word and answer that Voice, the Bible is an open invitation. "Listen!" says our Lord, "I am standing at the door knocking; if you hear my voice and open the door, I will come in to you and eat with you, and you with me" (Rev. 3:20).

Admittedly, the Reformed tradition historically has made some rather sweeping affirmations about the nature and authority of the Bible. So how do we honor these affirmations and at the same time understand the Bible in ways that speak God's redemptive Word directly to the trials and tribulations, the controversies and debates that we face today? And the first answer is that there is no easy answer. If there were an easy answer, we would all simply agree on everything that really matters and gladly agree to disagree agreeably on the things that do not matter. But such is not the case, and the question is not only fair but pressing: How do we responsibly interpret the scriptures?

One of the first things we must do is learn to read scripture in community. Now I realize that I am once again treading on thin ice because, in our culture, the individual's values and beliefs are an omnipresent trump card used to silence any and all challenges to one's personal views and lifestyle. After all, Sheilaism is all I need—just my own little voice. But I hope you will hear this, and hear it loud and clear. The Bible is not the private property of individuals; it is the Book of the community of faith. From the eyewitnesses of the mighty acts of God recorded in the Bible, to oral tradition, to the circulation of written texts, to the canonization of scripture, the Bible has been communicated to the people of God *in community* and then maintained by the community throughout the centuries.

Realizing that we are part of a universal community of believers stretching across all the generations from Abraham until now, we treat the texts of the Bible not as our private domain, to be used as a weapon against those with whom we disagree, but as voices of redemption, voices of challenge, voices of judgment, voices of promise, and voices of joy within that universal community. As we do so, one of the most critical aspects of Bible study is learning to ask the right questions. All too often, we impose on the text questions that the writers of the text never intended to answer, and more often than not when we do so, we know in advance the answer that we intend to get, even if we have to manipulate the text to get it. But honest biblical interpretation begins by letting the text speak on its own terms and from its own world because we seek to hear its ancient voice within the community that has interpreted it for centuries. In the Confession of 1967, we read,

> The Scriptures, given under the guidance of the Holy Spirit, are nevertheless the words of [people], conditioned by the language, thought forms, and literary fashions of the places and times at which they were written. They reflect views of life, history, and the cosmos which were then current. The church, therefore, has an obligation to approach the Scriptures with literary and historical understanding. . . .[17]

We open the Bible, of course, to hear a contemporary word from God in today's world, but we approach that contemporary word through the lens of the ancient community, as well as the community across the ages. It is difficult and sometimes impossible to determine the precise situation in life behind a text, but honest biblical study begins by grappling with the realities of the ancient community that gave us the text in the first place.

What would it mean then to ask the right questions of a text? A case in point is Genesis 1 and 2, which contain two accounts of God's creation of the universe and are often used to slug it out over creationism versus evolution. Everybody brings assumptions to the table, and one assumption often operative during this debate is that, for a person to be truly Christian, that person must fall in the camp of creationism. You've heard the argument: God created the world, quite literally, in six twenty-four-hour-days, and those who believe otherwise are obviously in error and have a lake of fire in their future. But what if . . . ? What if the writers of Genesis 1 and 2 were not attempting to make a historical or scientific comment, but a *theological claim*? What if the original audience of these two chapters were not plagued by questions of science and history but were languishing in a world they felt had kicked them in the teeth and left them bereft of grace and hungry for God? And what if the faithful in ages past chose to begin the Bible in this way not to offer a chronology or a historical account but to make a truthful claim about God and the faith to which God called them? Yes, what if they wrote these two chapters in order to build up the community of faith by affirming that God created the entire universe and everything in it and that God is the all-powerful Lord of life, who lovingly creates us for a divine purpose, and personally gives us life by blowing divine breath into our lungs? Do you see what an enormous difference is made by the questions we bring to a biblical text?

Some, of course, will insist that they don't "interpret" the Bible at all—that they instead simply read it word for word in the most literal sense. Their goal presumably is not to layer the Word with human interpretation but simply to take it in the literal form in which we have received it. But the fact is that the Word of God has been interpreted from time immemorial. Long before they were ever written down, the mighty acts of God recorded in the Bible were passed on by oral tradition from generation to generation. Literally, centuries passed before the sacred story of salvation was committed to writing, and each time it was repeated, it was interpreted afresh for *that* day and *those* circumstances, because our unchanging God was and is and always will be the ever-present Lord of life "though the earth should change," and "though the mountains shake in the heart of the sea" (Ps. 46:2). Is this not exactly what happens today in our homes and churches when the Bible is read? Everyone who seeks to understand the ancient texts of the Bible in the context of modern life interprets the Bible. No one takes everything in the Bible in a strictly literal sense. For example, in the Sermon on the Mount, Jesus says, "If your right eye causes you to sin, tear it out and throw it away. . . . And if your right hand causes you to sin, cut it off and throw it away; it is better for you to lose one of your members than for your whole body to go into hell" (Matt. 5:29–30). If we all took those verses literally, then the entire church would be without any eyes or hands. For who among us can honestly say that they have not sinned in what they have looked on with their eyes and in what they have done with their hands? But the last time I checked, the church was not eyeless and handless, so Jesus must have meant something other than taking a hacksaw to yourself as the best remedy for sin. Jesus was talking about the sin of adultery in those verses, and he was using hyperbole to get our attention and drive home a point in the most powerful, persuasive way possible.

Or consider for a moment this little caveat of our Lord. When we find him in the fourteenth chapter of Luke, the crowds are hunting him down mercilessly. In fact, they have become so infatuated with Jesus that they follow him everywhere. And in the midst of it, Jesus looks out at the crowd, and as far as the eye can see, there are would-be followers craving his presence. He suspects, though, that the push and shove of many of the enthusiasts amounts to no more than a short-lived obsession, sort of a Jesus craze that would be gone as soon as the wind shifted. So he chooses that moment to stop them dead in their tracks by saying, " 'Whoever comes to me and does not hate father and mother, wife and children, brothers and sisters, yes, and even life itself, cannot be my disciple'" (Luke 14:26). Surely, even the most committed literalists among us won't argue that Jesus meant literally that we are to harbor hate in our hearts for the very ones who brought us into the world and raised us, and for those with whom we live each day; that the very One who commanded us to " 'love one another as I have loved you'" (John 15:12) suddenly veered off the road of love only to plunge headlong into an ocean of hate. No, Jesus is telling everyone who wants to be his follower to stop and count the cost of discipleship. He is warning every enthusiast that following him will require more than enthusiasm; in fact, it will dramatically alter every aspect of life. "You want to follow me," says Jesus, "then make no mistake: Following me will change the way you think, the way you speak, the way you act, the way you behave with others, the friends you choose, and *literally* (for those who insist on being literal) *everything about you*. Oh, yes, and keep this in mind, too," Jesus continues. "Idolatry is a constant danger. In fact, you can make an idol even out of the people whom you love most in life. So watch out, be careful, think it through. This is not a job for casual volunteers."

Or consider this verse from the book of Leviticus: "All who curse father or mother shall be put to death; having cursed father or mother, their blood is upon them" (20:9). And then this: "If a man commits adultery with the wife of his neighbor, both the adulterer and the adulteress shall be put to death" (20:10). If we took such verses literally, most children wouldn't make it past adolescence, and the landscape would be littered with dead men and women whose hormones got the best of them one time too many. Furthermore, a literal reading of these verses would render the confession of sin obsolete and forgiveness entirely beside the point. I hope it goes without saying that I am not defending adultery as acceptable simply because it happens all the time, nor am I suggesting that all healthy children, even in the best of homes, curse their parents. But such verses as these help us to see that everyone makes interpretive choices. You and I may disagree with one another concerning the three passages I have just cited, but if we do so, it will be on the basis of interpretive choices we have made rather than the black (or red) ink we see forming certain words on the pages of the Bible.

In the eighth chapter of Acts, Philip, a disciple of Jesus, encounters an Ethiopian on the road from Jerusalem to Gaza. Noticing that the Ethiopian is reading the prophet Isaiah, Philip asks him, "Do you understand what you are reading?" to which the Ethiopian responds, "How can I, unless someone guides me?" or loosely translated, "How can I without someone to help me interpret what I am reading?"[18]

In Luke 24, the risen Christ meets Cleopas and another disciple on the road to Emmaus. It is Easter afternoon and the two of them are presumably taking the short walk to Emmaus in order to escape the terrible ordeal they have just been through. Jesus appears to them as a stranger on the road, and they proceed to unload on him everything that has just happened—how Jesus was a prophet mighty in word and deed, how he had been unjustly condemned to death and crucified, how some of the women among the followers of Jesus had astounded everyone by saying that his tomb was empty at dawn that morning. But Cleopas and the other disciple failed to understand the significance of these events until Jesus "interpreted to them the things about himself in all the scriptures" (24:27b). They had in their heads all the different pieces of the puzzle; they knew it like the back of their hand and could recite the entire tragic tale from A to Z. But none of it added up to anything significant or meaningful until the risen Lord interpreted it to them.

Reading Scripture in Community:
Listening to the Confessions

Biblical interpretation, however, is also shaped by another set of voices—those from the historic confessions of the church. This is the reason I have referred in these pages to various documents found in the *Book of Confessions*. Each of the confessions represents voices within the larger community of faith across the ages, reminding us that the gospel of Jesus Christ did not originate at dawn this morning and that we have much to learn from those who have gone before us. To be sure, the confessions are not on a par with holy scripture, but they hold a position of prominence and authority which Karl Barth has described like this:

> If Holy Scripture has binding authority, we cannot say the same of the Confessions. Yet there is still a non-binding authority, which must be taken

seriously. As our natural parents do not stand before us like God but nevertheless are in authority over us, so here too we have to do with a relative authority.[19]

I once heard Professor George Stroup describe the *Book of Confessions* as a kind of family picture album,[20] and that analogy has stuck with me in a helpful way through the years. Most of us have a family picture album in our homes, showing how we looked, how we dressed, and how our family has changed over a period of years. Throughout the album, the pictures reveal that the essential persons remained the same, but there were changes in appearance, changes in family composition, and perhaps even changes in the surroundings. In my own case, for example, being Steve Plunkett looks different today than it did in the 1950s, but the basic identity of the person is the same. Similarly, the *Book of Confessions* gives us a picture of what it has meant to be Christian and Reformed in various times and places, in various historical settings, and in various crises of faith, spanning the early centuries of the Christian era to the present time. And they represent voices from the past, both catholic and Reformed, which we need to hear and to heed as we interpret the Bible for the times in which we live. Barth describes an openness to those who have gone before us like this:

> If Holy Scripture alone is the divine teacher in the school in which we find ourselves ... we will not want to find ourselves in this school of the Church without fellow-pupils, without cooperation with them, without the readiness to be instructed by older and more experienced fellow-pupils. ... But if we hear it [Holy Scripture] as members of the Church, ... we do not hear the echo of the Word of God only or first of all in our own voice, but in the voice of others, those who were before us in the Church.[21]

Reading Scripture in Community:
Listening to Each Other Today

Interpreting the Bible in community, however, requires more than an openness to the ancient voices within scripture and the confessional heritage of the church. It also requires an openness to contemporary voices who also hunger to hear the Word of God afresh in our day. While reading the Bible in community may sound entirely sensible in theory, when it comes to navigating the storms of controversy, it can become a thorny issue indeed because *all individual interpretations are subject to the interpretation of the community as a whole.* No one person and no one advocacy group (or consortia thereof) within the church has the authority to determine the meaning of scripture for the whole church, which brings us to humility as a key ingredient of faithful Bible study. Here we have much to learn, for humility requires that every voice in the community be willing to listen to every other voice, because one of the primary ways we hear God speak in scripture is through each other. In writing about the authority of the Word, Barth addresses the need for humble openness to one another, suggesting that actual obedience to the authority of God's Word in holy scripture is determined, in significant measure, by whether or not we are "ready and willing to listen to one another in expounding and applying it."[22]

Interpreting the scriptures in community requires an enormous commitment to the church as a whole, a commitment so deep and strong that we are willing to set aside our personal interpretation if, when tested in the life of the community, that interpretation proves to be not in keeping with the Word of God. This to me is one of the tragic chapters in our life together. When I was growing up and, indeed as recently as when I was ordained, whenever a person joined the church, he or she was asked, "Do you subject yourself to your brothers and sisters in the Lord?" In that bygone era, subjection to one another in Jesus Christ was simply part of the fabric of the church's life. We didn't always "walk the walk," but we knew that this was the walk to which Christ called us, and we were clear that one very practical way of submitting to the lordship of Jesus Christ was through mutual subjection among those gathered at the foot of the cross. How shall we regain a sense of mutuality and humility in these contentious times apart from rediscovering the riches of God's grace in each other? For this is the only way to hear and obey the one Word of God we have been given in Jesus Christ. What do you think might happen if all the advocacy groups would stop their wrangling and politicking long enough to ask the question, "Is it possible that I am wrong?" Somehow we need to rediscover what it means to be gracious with each other, gracious enough to be "ready and willing to listen to one another." Barth is again helpful:

> But it is obvious that before I myself make a confession I must myself have heard the confession of the Church. . . . In my hearing and receiving of the Word of God I cannot separate myself from the Church to which it is addressed. I cannot thrust myself into the debate about a right faith which goes on in the Church without first having listened. . . . If my confession is to have weight in the Church, it must be weighted with the fact that I have heard the Church. If I have not heard the Church, I cannot speak to it. . . . How can I know Jesus Christ as the Lord who has called me by His Word if in relation to the rest of the Church I do not start from the thought that despite and in all the sin of [those] who constitute it it too has been called and ruled by the same Word?[23]

For this reason, Barth says that we enter debate in the church fully realizing it is "a debate in which I may have to be guided, or even opposed and certainly corrected."[24] Reading the Bible in community means approaching one another with such gracious humility.

Scripture Interprets Itself

There are times, of course, when the meaning of scripture is neither obscure nor ambiguous, and all the voices within the canon speak in unison. One of the dangers we face in the church today is choosing to become embroiled in controversy when the plain meaning of scripture is clear. Sometimes, though, the meaning of the Bible is not readily apparent, and in such times, Reformed Christians are guided in their interpretation of the Bible by remembering that *scripture interprets itself.* In the words of the Westminster Confession of Faith, "The infallible rule of interpretation of Scripture, is the Scripture itself; and therefore, when there is a question about the true and full sense of any scripture, . . . it may be searched and known by other places that speak more clearly."[25] You may have noticed that Presbyterians always seem to have an antenna out for proof-texting, that is, taking one slice of scripture and announcing imperiously, as if the final word is being spoken on the subject, "This is what the Bible says!" Rarely is it that easy. The full interpretation of scripture takes place when the various voices within scripture, voices that originated over hundreds and hundreds of years, are placed in conversation with one another, and when those voices, by the power of the Holy Spirit, are then placed in conversation with the times in which we live.

Two illustrations will help. In Leviticus 24:19, we read, "Anyone who maims another shall suffer the same injury in return: fracture for fracture, eye for eye, tooth for tooth; the injury inflicted is the injury to be suffered." In its original context, this so-called "law of retaliation" functioned in part as a prohibition against unrestrained revenge. An injured person should inflict no more injury on the offending party than he or she had suffered at the hands of the enemy. But let's face it; while this verse may once have placed boundaries on one's retaliatory actions, it is unquestionably about revenge, and if this were the only word in scripture on the subject, one might think we have been given carte blanche to inflict all manner of suffering on each other, and in the name of religion. But the fact is, there is indeed another voice within scripture on this very subject, and it is the voice of Jesus Christ: "You have heard that it was said, 'An eye for an eye and a tooth for a tooth.' But I tell you in the name of God that, if anyone strikes you on the right cheek, turn the other also" (Matt. 5:38–42). Here Jesus reminds us that the heart of God is not retribution in any circumstance, even when we are dealing with those who have hurt us. Rather, the heart of God is selfless mercy, and human relations are always something other than tit-for-tat, even though tit-for-tat may seem utterly fair (after all, she only got what was coming to her).

Or consider again the words of Jesus in Matthew 5:27–30 where the subject is adultery. The Ten Commandments are clear: You shall not commit adultery. Jesus, however, zeroes in on those who specialize in keeping the letter but not the spirit of the law because they are more interested in nice appearances than the interior life of the spirit. Jesus wants us to understand that, as far as God is concerned, many people are not guilty of adultery *except in their heart*. They don't actually get into bed with someone else's spouse, but they think about it, they picture it, they become sexually excited over the prospect, and they delight in their fantasy. And Jesus says, "If you have done that, then you have committed adultery, because keeping the commandments is supremely a matter of the heart."

Do you see the difference it makes to place various biblical voices in conversation with each other? One voice helps to clarify the other, rendering us a more complete understanding of God's purpose for our lives.

Spectacles of Faith

One of the most helpful ways I have found to understand scripture comes from John Calvin who wrote,

> Just as old or bleary-eyed men and those with weak vision, if you thrust before them a most beautiful volume, even if they recognize it to be some sort of writing, yet can scarcely construe two words, but with the aid of spectacles will begin to read distinctly; so Scripture, gathering up the otherwise confused knowledge of God in our minds, having dispersed our dullness, clearly shows us the true God.[26]

The older I get, the more meaningful I find these words of Calvin because, the older I become, the more dependent I am on my eyeglasses. Without them, the page of written text before me is nothing more than an indecipherable blur, but the moment I put on my prescription lenses, everything clears up. So it is with scripture. God is unknowable apart from the lens of the Bible. The world as God wants us to see it is an indecipherable blur without scripture. The neighbor who lives both beside us and across the planet is nothing but a terrifying enigma until we see the neighbor through the prescription lens God has given us in holy scripture.

Let me offer you a challenge. Think through all the major relationships in your life—your family, your coworkers, your friends, your church. But reflect also on the neighbor who struggles to make ends meet and seems always to be just one step ahead of the creditors. And think of the homeless Americans across this great nation of ours looking for help and searching for hope. When you see these brothers and sisters through the lens of holy scripture, do you see them differently? What about the cherished son or daughter who has entered the teenage years with a streak of terror you never dreamed you'd have to encounter, or the spouse you don't seem to know anymore? Does the lens of scripture help you to see them *as God wants you to see them*?

Feeding on the Word of God

When we see God, the world around us, and even ourselves through the lens of scripture, we are led to concrete acts of ministry that embody the love of Jesus Christ. As I have suggested, we don't read the Bible so our brains will become an impressive reservoir of biblical information. Rather, we read the Bible because we encounter Jesus Christ there and find in that encounter the grace we need to follow him across the perilous frontier of faith. Eugene Peterson commends the Bible as the very nourishment of God for the service of God in the world. Building on Revelation 10:9–10, Peterson suggests that our vocation in life is to "eat this Book." In other words, we are to consume the Word of God as divine nourishment for personal faith and obedience.

> Christians feed on Scripture. Holy Scripture nurtures the Holy Community as food nurtures the human body. Christians do not simply learn or study or use Scripture; we assimilate it, take it into our lives in such a way that it gets metabolized into acts of love, cups of cold water, missions into all the world, healing and evangelism and justice in Jesus' name, hands raised in adoration of the Father.[27]

The story is told of a Civil War chaplain, who one day encountered a wounded soldier on the battlefield. "Would you like to hear a few verses of scripture?" the chaplain asked the wounded man.

"No, sir," he answered, "but I'm thirsty. Could I please have some water?"

After giving him a drink of water, the chaplain asked again if he would like to hear some scripture, to which the wounded soldier replied, "No, sir, not now; but could you put something under my head?"

The chaplain did so, and repeated his question once more. "No, thank you," said the soldier. "But I'm cold. Could you cover me up?"

At this point, the chaplain took off his greatcoat and placed it over the wounded man. By now, he was afraid to ask again about the reading of scripture, so he started to walk away. But the soldier called to him, "Look, Chaplain, if there's anything in that book of yours that makes a person do for another what you've done for me, then I want to hear it."[28]

The Bible nourishes us to make a concrete connection between our faith in God and the needs all around us. May God grant us divine grace to feed on scripture. May we learn, by the inward testimony of the Holy Spirit, to bring our lives under the scrutiny of God's Word—our homes, our families, our jobs, our churches, our sexuality, our social relationships, our ethics, and especially the deepest devotion of our hearts. And may we learn, by God's grace, to apply the Bible to our lives *and* our lives to the Bible.

Truth 7

We Are the Church Together

Now you are the body of Christ and individually members of it.
(1 Cor. 12:27)

Pentecost: The Church Is Born

The story of the church begins with an explosion that would forever change the world—not an explosion created by human hands or engineered by human calculation, but a spiritual explosion of the living God more powerful than any human imagining. If you have never done so, now would be a good time to read the first two chapters of the book of Acts. As the risen Lord was about to ascend into heaven, he promised the disciples that, very soon, the Holy Spirit would fill them with the power of the resurrection. The incomparable power that once brooded over the face of the deep (Gen. 1:1) and created beauty and order out of chaos was about to burst forth on the followers of Jesus. The same power that caused the dead Jesus, cold in the tomb, to rise up and live again was on the verge of creating a new and emboldened community to proclaim the gospel to every far-flung corner of God's creation. Now the story of God's redemptive love will be told in every tongue and proclaimed in every culture. And the good news that "God so loved the world that he gave his only Son" (John 3:16) will inspire the disciples of Jesus to unthinkable acts of sacrifice and service. But, for now, Jesus instructed them to go into Jerusalem and wait for the gift of the Holy Spirit.

When the day of Pentecost arrived, Jews from all over the known world were in Jerusalem to celebrate the Feast of Weeks that fell on the fiftieth day after Passover. This was an annual feast celebrating the harvest, and in later times, the giving of the law by Moses was also commemorated.[1] It was a holy moment for the Jews gathered in Jerusalem, but little did they know that God was poised to unleash the Holy Spirit with a power the likes of which they had never imagined.

In the midst of the feast, the followers of Jesus were together in one place. Suddenly, the rush of a violent wind from heaven filled the house where they were sitting; tongues as of fire appeared and rested on each of them; and they all "were filled with the Holy Spirit and began to speak in other languages, as the Spirit gave them ability." It was an explosion of power so potent and alien to ordinary human experience that everyone present was baffled and astonished. For there were people in Jerusalem from every nation under heaven, and they all heard the disciples speaking in their native language. "How can this be?" they asked. "Are not all these ordinary Galileans?" Some of them were filled with utter awe and wonder, but others scoffed and made light of it, saying, "These crazy people are drunk" (Acts 2:1–4).

This peculiar story of the power of God is the story of the church's birthday. And the first lesson of Pentecost is that the Holy Spirit cannot be tamed, for the Holy Spirit is full of surprises beyond all human imagination and is so powerful that ordinary human beings have their lives totally turned around. Filled with the Holy Spirit, Peter preached the gospel in the streets of Jerusalem, and three thousand people, that very day, were baptized and added to the believing community. Who would have expected it? This, after all, was the same Peter who denied Jesus three times on the night of his arrest. Peter didn't expect it. The crowd didn't expect it. It was totally *God's* doing through the indomitable power of the Holy Spirit. Neither did anyone expect the apostles to perform signs and wonders so powerful that the inhabitants of Jerusalem were filled with awe and wonder. It was beyond human hope, beyond human comprehension. Certainly, no one expected this small band of believers in a crucified troublemaker to spread the gospel throughout the known world. And no one expected a man named Saul, the most embittered and zealous of Christian-haters, to become a champion of the Christian way and end up suffering shipwreck, imprisonment, and beatings because of his faith in Jesus Christ.[2] Yet all of this happened by the surprising, untamable Spirit of the living God.

Yet the story of Pentecost also makes another brave declaration: *The church is God's community, not ours.* Sometimes, amid the squabbles of church life, we begin to think that the church belongs to us—don't we?—and that it is ours to manage as we choose. But if Pentecost stands for anything at all, it stands for this: The church of Jesus Christ belongs to no governing body, no pastor, no committee, and no "right" way of thinking. The church was not crafted by a task force or by a General Assembly action, and neither was it engineered to serve any human agenda. It is not the property of any denomination or the possession of any movement whether it be tagged liberal or conservative, moderate or centrist, left-wing or right-wing. The church, wonder of wonders, is *God's* possession, despite every wart and blemish that we humans bring to it. It is nothing less than the redemptive body of Jesus Christ poured out in divine love for all creation.

Anyone who has spent much time taking part in the life of the church knows, however, that the church is also a thoroughly human community. Sometimes we stumble and fall, and more often than not, the life of the church is punctuated by false starts and wrong turns. Yet the church is a community that carries in its soul the promise of forgiveness and the incomparable joy of belonging to Jesus Christ. So the most frightening danger is not a false start or a wrong turn, but the prospect that we will stop listening for the voice of Jesus Christ in scripture and try to live by our own power rather than by the life-changing wind of the Holy Spirit.

Airborne or Grounded?

When we reflect on the life of the church today through the lens of Acts 2, some piercing questions arise. In fact, you may be thinking, "That isn't like any congregation *I've* ever been part of!" Indeed, where is the evidence that today's church is driven by the same raw, untamed power that we encounter in the story of Pentecost? Perhaps it would be helpful, before going further, to reflect on some of the realities of congregational life in our time.

I am constantly amazed at the pressing need in the church of a lively sense of vision. And I would be willing to bet that, when it comes to our personal sense of vision for the future of the church, we don't envision the likes of a violent wind and flaming tongues of fire and the unrestrained power of God unleashed right in the midst of Presbyterian decency and order. No, I suspect that the picture in our heads is of a church that is much more timid, much more tentative.

In his excellent book *High-Flying Geese*, Browne Barr reminds us of the case of Søren Kierkegaard's wild goose who went to live with a flock of tame geese:

> He was resolved to liberate them from their domesticated life of mediocrity, where the food was rich and life was easy although dull and limited by the farmer's grim ultimate purposes. He lived there until he himself was tame.
>
> Every year, when the other geese would honk in flight overhead, he would flutter his wings and rise a bit and resolve to join them, but he never did, finally becoming content to be with the tamed and flightless birds.[3]

As Barr suggests, God wants the church of Jesus Christ to be airborne by the power of the Holy Spirit and to soar with divine purpose. But all too often we become grounded, and soon we become so tamed by the world around us that we are content to be like flightless birds who have abandoned their destiny. We do a good bit of honking from time to time in our congregations. We even flutter our wings and give off the distinct impression that we fully intend to become airborne, but somehow it never really happens. Barr also tells the story of another flock of geese found in the writings of Kierkegaard:

> The sermon was essentially the same each time. It told of the glorious destiny of geese, of the noble end for which their maker had created them— and every time his name was mentioned the geese curtsied and all the ganders bowed their heads. They were to use their wings to fly away to the distant pastures to which they really belonged; for they were only pilgrims on this earth.
>
> The same thing happened each Sunday. Thereupon the meeting broke up and they all waddled home, only to meet again next Sunday for divine worship and waddle off home again—but that was as far as they ever got. They throve and grew fat, plump and delicious—and at Michaelmas they were eaten—and that was as far as they ever got.[4]

Kierkegaard's illustration is a caricature, to be sure, but it is not without the clear ring of familiarity. Far too often, we succeed in whittling the church down to a manageable size with a manageable budget that doesn't challenge anybody too much or confront the tiny picture in our heads of the call to service. We are rather like T. S. Eliot's J. Alfred Prufrock, who laments, "I have measured out my life with coffee spoons."[5]

To get a sense of the broad scope of the Bible's vision of the church, consider this statement from the *Book of Order*: "The Church of Jesus Christ is the provisional demonstration of what God intends for all of humanity."[6] There are no coffee spoons in that vision of the church, and no grounded geese, only the people of God airborne by the unmanageable power of the Holy Spirit. The gospel's canvas is indeed large, as large as all creation. Paul writes,

> With all wisdom and insight [God] has made known to us the mystery of his will, according to his good pleasure that he set forth in Christ, as a plan for the fullness of time, to gather up all things in him, things in heaven and things on earth. (Eph. 1:8b–10)

Indeed, God's purpose in Jesus Christ is as broad and expansive as the cosmos: *to gather up all things in him.* And the vocation of the church is to play a servant role in this divine purpose. In a world marred by hatred and bigotry and every conceivable brand of party spirit, the church is to bear witness to God's new creation in which the brokenness of human life is healed, sin against God and neighbor is forgiven, reconciliation between warring factions is accomplished, and the dividing walls of hatred between human beings are demolished.[7] This is the joy to which we have been called.

Here again, however, when we place this grand vision of the church up against the realities of congregational life, we find ourselves back with Prufrock's coffee spoons. I am constantly amazed, for example, at how often I run into the notion that the church is comparable to all the volunteer organizations in town, such as the Lions Club or Rotary or Kiwanis. Try to find *that* in the book of Acts, or anywhere in the New Testament, and you come up empty-handed. The church of Jesus Christ is totally distinct from all other human associations. Giving money to the church is never the same as giving money to the United Fund or donating one's time to the public library or the local PTA. Without question, all of these endeavors are important and they enrich the lives of many communities. But let us be clear about this one thing: *The church of Jesus Christ is totally distinct from all other human organizations, societies, and commitments.*

Years ago, I was sought out by a gentleman who was wrought up about the life of his congregation. Things weren't going his way. No matter how much he did for the church, he didn't feel appreciated, and, for him, the tell-tale sign of appreciation was getting his way. "You know," he said, "I'm the sort of person who always needs a pet project. For a while, it was running the booster club at the high school, and then it was teaching English as a second language, but for the past couple of years, the church has been my pet project." While there may have been several wrongheaded notions at work in this individual's approach to the life of the church, chief among them was the idea of the church as his pet project. The church is not anybody's pet project. The community that was born through the power of a violent wind and tongues of fire simply is not that small, that trivial, that paltry. Instead, the church is the body of Jesus Christ for our wounded world, and, as such, it is the community that lives to serve *God's* agenda, which is as big as all creation. Yet the conversation I have just recalled typifies the mind-set that many people bring with them into the pew. It is a mind-set that liberally feeds the belief that the church is there for me and my family, and that joining a particular congregation has to do not with the service I am called to render to God and my neighbor but with what that congregation has to offer me and my family in the way of enriching (and in some cases, entertaining) programs. As a pastor, I experience the "pet project" mentality in a variety of ways, one of the most prominent being the expectation that the church is a spiritual smorgasbord of goods and services that should strike just the perfect balance between entertainment and substance. It's as though the church were a gigantic supermarket where we all get to pick and choose our beliefs just like we choose between iceberg lettuce and spinach, yellow squash and zucchini—it's all a matter of personal taste and choice. The Canadian sociologist Reginald Bibby has called this approach to the church "religion à la carte."[8] And David F. Wells illustrates it well by suggesting that, in our situation today, "the self circumscribes the significance of Christian faith," so that

> good and evil are reduced to a sense of well-being or its absence, God's place in the world is reduced to the domain of private consciousness, his external acts of redemption are trimmed to fit the experience of personal salvation, his providence in the world diminishes to whatever is necessary to ensure one's having a good day, his Word becomes intuition, and conviction fades into evanescent opinion. Theology becomes therapy, and all the telltale symptoms of the therapeutic model of faith begin to surface. The biblical interest in righteousness is replaced by a search for happiness, holiness by wholeness, truth by feeling, ethics by feeling good about one's self. The world shrinks to the range of personal circumstances; the community of faith shrinks to a circle of personal friends. The past recedes. The Church recedes. All that remains is the self.[9]

This, of course, is a denial of the church's fundamental identity and calling. So to glimpse more fully that identity and calling, we turn now to one of the most basic realities of our life together: the covenant God has made with us in Jesus Christ. For whatever else we may be as the church, we are the covenant community of the sovereign God.

A Community Rooted in Covenant

The Bible's concept of covenant is firmly rooted in the Old Testament and closely related to the doctrine of election (see discussion in "Truth 2"). Indeed, it was God's electing grace that created the covenant community through Abraham and Sarah and their descendants. In the Old Testament, the Hebrew word for "covenant" appears 286 times, in addition to numerous other references to covenant relationships where the word itself does not occur.[10] It is impossible to overstate the importance of the covenant in understanding the essential identity of the people of God. In the most general sense, a covenant is a contract, an agreement into which various parties enter by making promises to each other. Indeed, the covenant found in the Bible is not one between equals but between unequals, in which the Lord of the universe freely enters into a special covenant relationship with the community of faith for the good of all creation. God promises divine faithfulness to the covenant community and pledges the assurance of divine love, guidance, and protection. And in return, the covenant community promises to live in covenant faithfulness to the God who called it into being. In essence, God makes the unfailing promise, "I shall be your God," and then issues the inescapable command, "And you shall live as my people."

In the Old Testament, the idea of covenant is seen in a variety of ways. God establishes a covenant with Adam and Eve in the Garden of Eden, with Noah in Genesis 8, with Abraham in Genesis 12, and with the nation of Israel at the foot of Mount Sinai. Throughout Israel's life, the two tablets of the law (Ten Commandments) are specifically understood as tablets *of the covenant* and, early on, circumcision becomes the sign of inclusion in the covenant community as well as the rite of passage into the community. It is also worth noting that, as the Israelites finally take possession of the promised land, Joshua gathers all the tribes together at Shechem for a ceremony of covenant renewal. In Israel's later life, the call to covenant faithfulness is a constant thread running throughout the prophets, who never tire of reminding the Israelites that their problems are rooted in the fact that they have turned their backs on the covenant that God made with their ancestors at Mount Sinai.

In the New Testament, Jesus Christ himself is the bond of God's covenant love. The prophet Jeremiah had promised that God would one day make a new covenant with Israel:

> It will not be like the covenant that I made with their ancestors when I took them by the hand to bring them out of the land of Egypt—a covenant that they broke. . . . But this is the covenant that I will make with the house of Israel, says the Lord: I will put my law within them, and I will write it on their hearts; and I will be their God, and they shall be my people. No longer shall they teach one another, or say to each other, 'Know the Lord,' for they shall all know me, from the least of them to the greatest, says the Lord; for I will forgive their iniquity, and remember their sin no more. (Jer. 31:31–34)

Jeremiah promised a covenant that would be planted in the very depths of the human heart, and in this new covenant, all of God's good intentions for the human race would finally be realized. Then, on the night before his crucifixion, as our Lord shares the cup with his disciples, he says, "This cup that is poured out for you is the new covenant in my blood" (Luke 22:20). Our relationship with the sovereign God of the universe is possible because of the covenant God has made with us in Jesus Christ, and the church is the community of that covenant. Indeed, one of the primary ways to understand the sacrament of Holy Communion is as a ceremony of covenant renewal. And in the life of the early church, the sacrament of baptism became what circumcision had been in Judaism, namely, the sign of inclusion in the covenant community.

The "Called Out" People of God:
Disciples in the Making

This understanding of God's covenant love and the call to covenant faithfulness brings us to a word that figures prominently in the New Testament. *Ecclesia* is the Greek word for "church," occurring some 112 times in the New Testament[11] and representing a vital connection with the themes of covenant and election. The *ecclesia* of God literally refers to a people called out of the world to render service to God. To say that the church is "called out" does not mean that the Christian community is somehow set above the rest of the world, comfortably removed from the thorns and thistles of life. Rather, the *ecclesia* of God is called out of the world in order to be equipped for service, and then sent back into the world to speak and live as the community of God's covenant love.

The Christian community, therefore, nourishes the "called out" people of God to go into all the world as ambassadors for Christ. For this reason, John Calvin refers to the church, in a striking way, as our *mother*. Just as God is our Heavenly Father, so also the church is our mother and, therefore, an indispensable part of every believer's relationship with Jesus Christ. According to Calvin, the church nurses at the church's (mother's) breast in order to be nourished for service to God. He writes,

> I shall start, then, with the church, into whose bosom God is pleased to gather his [children], not only that they may be nourished by her help and ministry as long as they are infants and children, but also that they may be guided by her motherly care until they mature and at last reach the goal of faith . . . so that, for those to whom he is Father the church may also be Mother. . . .
>
> For there is no other way to enter into life unless this mother conceive us in her womb, give us birth, nourish us at her breast, and . . . keep us under her care and guidance. . . . Our weakness does not allow us to be dismissed from her school until we have been pupils all our lives.[12]

Calvin's high view of the church is a far cry from religion à la carte. Not many people today understand that their faith is actually dependent on the spiritual nourishment that flows from the mother church to each believer. The typical attitude toward the church is much more casual, because the church, after all, is a discretionary aspect of faith, not an indispensable one. Here we need to tread with particular care, lest we make the church itself into an idol. We again turn to Shirley Guthrie who helps us understand the way in which the church is essential:

> It is not the church but the God whom we come to know in Christ who saves. Although it is true that the church is bound to Christ, it is not true that Christ

is trapped in the church. He came to express God's love not just for Christians and the church but for all people, for the whole world. He is the risen Lord who is at work not only in the church but everywhere, even among people who do not recognize or acknowledge his liberating, reconciling, healing work. . . .What we can say is that although God is not bound to the church, we Christians are bound to it. That is where the Christ who is at work in loving and liberating power everywhere is specifically known, thankfully trusted, and voluntarily served.[13]

We Christians are bound to the church because the "called out" people of God need the life-giving nourishment that only our mother can give, and we need this nourishment in order to be made into faithful disciples of Jesus Christ. We are not a happy-go-lucky camaraderie of like-minded volunteers, but a disciplined community of disciples in the making. We have not yet "arrived," but we are on the way because the church is a community where followers of Jesus are taught and shaped and corrected and forgiven and nurtured and challenged and trained and loved.

To glimpse this more fully, turn to Luke 9:51–62. Twice we are told in these verses that Jesus "set his face toward Jerusalem," which is New Testament shorthand for saying that Jesus was on his way to the cross. As they are walking along, a would-be follower of Jesus approaches him and says, "Lord, I've heard your preaching and I've witnessed the marvelous signs of God that you perform, and I know I'll never desert you; I promise to follow you wherever you go!" But Jesus senses that his promise is no more than a sudden burst of enthusiasm without any enduring commitment behind it, so he says, "Wait a minute. You don't know what you're saying. I think you better count the cost of discipleship. Foxes have holes to sleep in, and birds of the air have nests. But I have nowhere to lay my head at night. Are you sure you are ready for that kind of life?"

A few minutes later, Jesus says to another person, "Come, follow me." But this would-be follower thinks he has a foolproof excuse. "I really want to join you, but first let me bury my father." One would think that his father had recently died and that he was asking at most for a few days to set his affairs in order. But Kenneth Bailey teaches us that this interpretation misunderstands the text and is foreign to its Middle Eastern culture. He suggests that "Let me go and bury" means "Let me go serve my father until he dies at some point in the future, who knows when; then after I bury him, I'll come and follow."[14] And to his delay tactics Jesus offers a stern warning: "Let the dead bury the dead; but as for you, *now* is the time to go and proclaim the kingdom of God."

A third would-be follower then says to Jesus, "I want to follow you, Lord, but first let me go home and say my goodbyes." Surely Jesus wouldn't begrudge the man his goodbyes. But Jesus sees in his response an indecision and says to him, "*Today* is the day of decision; *now* is the time to follow."

The church is the company of those who have heard the *today* of Christ's call and have responded with the *now* of commitment. And our mother, the church, nourishes us with the gifts of grace that we need to follow faithfully.

The Body of Christ:
"Blest Be the Tie That Binds"

One of the hardest things to get through our thick skulls in the North American context is the concept of the church as a *body*, a *community*, a *collective* organism. We follow Jesus Christ not as an assortment of individualists committed to the tenets of rugged individualism but as the *body* of Jesus Christ in the world. And we begin our discussion of the communal nature of the church with the gifts of God bountifully given for the common good. One of Paul's most eloquent passages is the twelfth chapter of 1 Corinthians where he assures us that God has given the church every conceivable gift needed for faithfulness to Jesus Christ:

> Now there are varieties of gifts, but the same Spirit; and there are varieties of services, but the same Lord; and there are varieties of activities, but it is the same God who activates all of them in everyone. To each is given the manifestation of the Spirit for the common good. (1 Cor. 12:4–7)

And to the Ephesians, he writes in a similar vein:

> The gifts he gave were that some would be apostles, some prophets, some evangelists, some pastors and teachers, to equip the saints for the work of ministry, for building up the body of Christ. (Eph. 4:11–12)

What are your gifts for ministry? What has God given you to share with your brothers and sisters in Christ *for the common good*? Many parishioners believe that the gifts for ministry have been reserved for those who go to seminary and enter the ministry as a vocation. But nothing could be further from the truth, and, to be honest, this is one of the most frequent frustrations I face as a pastor. Whether it's time to nominate new elders and deacons or to recruit committee members or to secure Sunday school teachers or youth group sponsors, a common litany heard around the church is, "I can't do that. . . . I don't have enough time. . . . That's not something I'm good at. . . . Look around at all the capable people; ask one of them!" But the gospel assures us that every believer in Jesus Christ has been given the gifts of God for the corporate ministry of the church. No one has been left out. All are included. And one of the greatest needs of today's church is uncovering the generous treasure of gifts God has graciously given to the community of faith.

The use of our individual gifts in the service of Jesus Christ leads us directly into the corporate life of the community of faith. Part of the marvelous grace of God is that, as we use our gifts together, we experience the joy of being part of the body of Christ. It may be difficult to grasp the full intent of Paul's analogy in the face of our stout American individualism, but Paul continues the passage about gifts by comparing the church to a human body, and he even goes so far as to say that disciples of Christ are every bit as interconnected as the diverse parts of the human body. Picture it in your mind's eye. We are as intimately and intricately connected as the fingers are to the hand, and the hand to the wrist, and the wrist to the arm, and the arm to the shoulder, and the shoulder to the torso, and all of it to the brain. In other words, *we all need each other for faithfulness to Jesus Christ, because no one can do it alone*. The church is not an association of autonomous lone rangers. No one can be faithful to God in isolation from the body of Christ, and to attempt to do so is the most egregious expression of hubris. My faithfulness to God is not on my shoulders alone, for it is also on your shoulders, and your faithfulness, likewise, is on my shoulders. We are just that interconnected. We are a *body*, a *community* of the risen Lord. In part, this means that Christ calls us to bear one another's joys and sorrows. But it also means that, because we have not all been given the same gifts for ministry, we are dependent on the complementary gifts of each other to do the work of Christ.

Look around you the next time you are in worship and consider the very human implications of Paul's theology. Our need for each other nudges us toward an uncommon humility because being the body of Christ together means that we actually *need* the irritating person sitting across the sanctuary, the know-it-all sitting two pews over, the one who seems aloof and standoffish, the person who was totally annoying at the last committee meeting. And wonder of wonders, it means that there is even a place for you and me with all of our annoying idiosyncrasies! Just as the hand is connected to the foot through the life of the body, so also the community of faith. Through baptism, we have been engrafted into the body of Christ. In committing ourselves to Christ, we have committed ourselves for all eternity to the community of forgiven sinners gathered at the foot of the cross. And notice the inescapable *you* of Paul's affirmation: "Now you are the body of Christ and individually members of it" (1 Cor. 12:27).

While the notion of the church as a corporate entity may challenge many of the cultural assumptions that we bring into the sanctuary on Sunday mornings, it also is an immensely comforting image of the church. For if the church is indeed an authentic community, then we do stand with and by and for one another as we face the storms of life. "If one member suffers," writes Paul, "all suffer together with it; if one member is honored, all rejoice together with it" (1 Cor. 12:26). This came home to me in a particularly poignant and moving way during the illness and death of both of my parents. In both instances, my personal feelings of loss were heightened by the number of miles that physically separated us. So I was unable to be the kind of help I wanted to be during their illnesses. Much to my comfort, one profound expression of God's amazing grace was the way that the members of my congregation read between the lines and knew exactly what I was feeling—my personal hurt at watching my parents waste away, one physically, the other mentally; my disappointment that I couldn't be with them more often to give back some of the nurture and love they had both given me so constantly; and my guilt over feeling that I wasn't carrying my share of the burden. Some of those in my congregation knew from inside their own souls what I was experiencing because they themselves had been there. They personally had walked on those thorns and navigated those horrors with their own parents or other loved ones. They, too, had watched through the flow of tears as a loved one's journey came to that final crossroads and entered the valley of the shadow of death. And the gift of grace that some of them gave me was the grace of knowing that they had been there and that somehow we were *together* in a common experience. That is the church being the church. That is a ragtag conglomeration of individual Christians becoming a *community*, a *collective* organism, the *body* of Jesus Christ in a wounded world. And that is the joy of belonging both to God and to each other. The old hymn "Blest Be the Tie That Binds" says it this way:

> We share our mutual woes,
> Our mutual burdens bear,
> And often for each other flows
> The sympathizing tear.[15]

John Killinger tells the story of a woman from the Shenandoah Valley of Virginia. She was a painter, and one day she took her canvas and paint into the woods. As she sat there painting a scene, two shots suddenly rang out, and she was hit. There were two young men on a nearby bluff with a rifle, and they continued firing at her until she was struck, first, on the hand, then on one of her thighs and in the torso. That's all she remembers happening before she passed out. By the time she was found, she had lost so much blood and was in such a state of shock that her doctors advised against immediate surgery. They waited nearly a week for her to stabilize to the point that they felt they could subject her body to the added trauma of surgery. Most of that week, she lay hovering between life and death. Her body was suspended above the bed in a sling, and while she experienced only intermittent consciousness, one part of the experience is indelibly etched in her memory. People from her church, which she attended only irregularly, took care of her. They came in shifts to sit with her, to love her, to pray for her. She couldn't speak, and they didn't even know for certain that she knew they were present, but they stayed anyway. The woman, in fact, recovered and later said of those days in the hospital:

> I lay there in a sling, blissfully aware of their coming and going. I felt as if I were cradled in a cocoon of love. It didn't matter if I lived or died. I was part of the beloved community.[16]

Such is life in the body of Christ. "If one member suffers, all suffer together with it; if one member is honored, all rejoice together with it." Do you have anything inside of you that could help your congregation be that kind of community? "To each is given the manifestation of the Spirit for the common good."

A Servant People Following a Servant Lord

The church, however, does not exist for its own sake but for the sake of all creation. Jesus said, "Go therefore and make disciples of all nations, baptizing them in the name of the Father and of the Son and of the Holy Spirit, and teaching them to obey everything that I have commanded you" (Matt. 28:19). Being the body of Christ to each other within the fellowship of faith is never the end of the matter, for Christ also calls us to be his body *in the world* where people are hurting and aching for hope. Every day, concrete human needs take people to the threshold of despair. Some are crushed by the brutality of abuse. Some suffer the indignities of having no place to lay their head at night, no home to call their own, no safe haven for their children to experience the security that so many of us take for granted. And others are simply hungry and in need of the kindness of a hot meal. One day, I visited with a man who eats regularly in a local soup kitchen operated by a number of congregations in our community, and he told me that the soup kitchen was an answer to prayer because without it he is reduced to rummaging through various dumpsters around town. In such a world as this, the redemptive community of Jesus Christ is called to the "holy discontent" of the gospel. We are called not to be silent, but to speak out, because we know the world is not the way God intended it to be. Albert Curry Winn helps us to see the dangers of being too inwardly focused:

> Of course a church has services to render to its own members. They have great needs. They are ignorant and must be taught the foundations of faith— Christian education. They are apathetic and must be aroused—preaching.

They are bruised and wounded by life and must be healed—pastoral work. They are in each other's way and need organizing—administration. All these ye ought to have done!

The question is, Where is the priority? Where is most of the time of church members spent when they do what they call "church work"? Are they out in the world in the work of proclamation, justice, compassion, and peace? Or are they oiling the ecclesiastical machinery? Examine the church budget. How many dollars go to serve the needs of the world, and how many to maintain the institution of the church? Have we gone out into the world in any meaningful way, or are we still hiding in the sanctuary?[17]

The New Testament vision of the church's life, of course, has nothing to do with hiding in the sanctuary and everything to do with reaching out, in the name of Jesus Christ, to all creation. *For the church is a servant people following a servant Lord.* One of the most powerful passages in the Bible is the Christ hymn in the second chapter of Philippians where Paul insists that our identity as the body of Christ is rooted in and shaped by Christ's journey to the cross:

> Let the same mind be in you that was in Christ Jesus,
> who, though he was in the form of God,
> did not regard equality with God
> as something to be exploited,
> but emptied himself,
> taking the form of a slave,
> being born in human likeness.
> And being found in human form,
> he humbled himself
> and became obedient to the point of death—
> even death on a cross.
> Therefore God also highly exalted him
> and gave him the name
> that is above every name,
> so that at the name of Jesus
> every knee should bend,
> in heaven and on earth and under the earth,
> and every tongue should confess
> that Jesus Christ is Lord,
> to the glory of God the Father.
>
> (Phil. 2:5–11)

If, however, our calling is to follow the servant Lord, the character and content of our service is *love*. Jesus said, "This is my commandment, that you love one another as I have loved you" (John 15:12). Then in John 21, he gives us a picture of what he means by "love." The disciples have spent an entire night fishing in the Sea of Tiberias. It is now just after daybreak, and they have absolutely nothing to show for their night of labor, only empty nets. Jesus stands on the beach, but the disciples do not recognize him. Seeing that they have no fish, he tells them to cast their net on the other side of the boat, and suddenly their net is so full that they are unable to haul in their catch. The disciples then realize that they are in the presence of the risen Lord, and they go ashore. After breakfast, Jesus says to Simon Peter,

> "Simon, son of John, do you love me more than these?" [Peter] said to him, "Yes, Lord; you know that I love you." Jesus said to him, "Feed my lambs." A second time [Jesus] said to him, "Simon, son of John, do you love me?" [Peter] said to him, "Yes, Lord; you know that I love you." Jesus said to him, "Tend my sheep." He said to him the third time, "Simon son of John, do you love me?" (John 21:15–17a)

Now Peter is hurt because Jesus has questioned his love three times. Exasperated, he says, "Lord, you know everything; you know that I love you." "Then feed my sheep," says the risen Lord.

This short exchange between Jesus and Peter contains the job description for the community of faith. "Do you love me?" Jesus asks each of us (not only as individuals but collectively as a community). And with Peter, we answer, "Yes, Lord, we have committed our lives to you." And the sovereign word of Jesus is, "Then love each other; take care of my world." We gather for worship on Sunday mornings and say to Jesus, "Lord, thank you for your love; we are grateful to be forgiven." And Jesus answers us, "Then take my gospel outside the doors of the church and minister to your wounded neighbors. Transform the structures of society that exploit the poor and trample on human need. If you truly love me, then show it by loving others."

Word and Sacrament

These words of our Lord are enough to make us ask, "How is this kind of life possible?" And the only answer I know is this: The faithfulness to which Jesus calls us is a sheer miracle of God's grace. Like salvation itself, it is impossible to generate faithfulness on our own steam. It is a kind of life that we can only receive with joy and gratitude from the hands of Another. And because we are helpless to do it on our own, we look to our mother, the church, for nourishment and strength. We gather ourselves around the Word of God and the sacraments of grace in order to be nourished for the life to which we are called. John Calvin once wrote,

> Wherever we see the Word of God purely preached and heard, and the sacraments administered according to Christ's institution, there, it is not to be doubted, a church of God exists.[18]

The church is a peculiar community indeed, gathered around the proclamation of Jesus Christ, crucified and risen, and the celebration of the sacraments of baptism and Holy Communion. As we encounter Jesus Christ in Word and sacrament, by the grace of God, our old self begins to die and the new self is born. As the Word of God is read and preached, the gift of God's new creation in Jesus Christ begins to break into our stubborn selves, and the undying passions of the Holy Spirit begin to thaw our cold hearts. As we encounter the living Christ in the waters of baptism, the realities of faithful love begin to dawn inside us. And as the crucified and risen One comes to us in the bread and cup of Holy Communion, we learn the incomparable joy of keeping company with the Savior of the world.

This is why the regular gathering of the community for worship is so critical to our spiritual health. Our mother church uses the preaching of the Word and the celebration of the sacraments to nourish us for life together under the reign of God. The preaching of the Word conveys to us all the promises of God, and baptism and Holy Communion seal those promises on our consciences:[19] the promise that the sovereign God of the universe is truly in charge of our lives; the promise that God has called an elect people to be a blessing to all creation; the promise that the ugliness of sin does not have the last word over us, because Jesus Christ died on the cross and rose from the grave to forgive us; the promise that the Bible is indeed "a lamp to our feet and a light to our path" (Ps. 119:105) in all the ache and confusion of life; the promise that we do not have to prove ourselves worthy of God's love because God loves us despite our worst selves; the promise that the grace of the Holy Spirit changes us into persons of selfless love for God and neighbor; the promise that the Holy Spirit never tires of picking us up when we fall and helping us to stand again; the promise of eternal life because death no longer holds us captive; the promise that we are included in a worldwide communion of all the faithful who, in every age, have been part of God's covenant community.

The Holy Catholic Church

The explosion of power with which the book of Acts begins was an explosion so great that its effects are still being felt today. The Holy Spirit has been at work in every generation, proclaiming Christ's message of love and calling human beings of every land and tongue into the kingdom of God. The good news is that we are indeed part of a universal community made up of all those who, throughout the ages, have professed their faith in Jesus Christ as Lord and Savior.[20] By the grace of God, the faith community is "elect from every nation, yet one o'er all the earth."[21] This community is neither Presbyterian nor Protestant. It is catholic, in that it is a universal, worldwide community of believers. This is what the Apostles' Creed means by affirming our inclusion in "the holy catholic church." The gospel assures us that the church is not as small as one congregation, presbytery, or denomination. Rather, *all* Christians in *all* times and places are connected to each other in the fellowship of the church. As Paul wrote to the Ephesians, "There is one body and one Spirit, just as you were called to the one hope of your calling, one Lord, one faith, one baptism, one God and Father of all, who is above all and through all and in all" (Eph. 4:4–6).

This is the gracious, good news of the gospel as we join our hands and hearts and voices in the worship and service of God. This is the good cheer that Jesus Christ has given to us. This is the surpassing joy that comes from the throne of grace—a joy that the world cannot give, a joy that can only come from the generous hand of God. Surely, our lives are rooted in this joy. And just as surely, our faith is grounded in the loving promise that God "chose us in Christ before the foundation of the world to be holy and blameless before him in love"; that God "destined us for adoption as his children through Jesus Christ"; and that, through the redemption of the cross, God has made us part of "a plan for the fullness of time, to gather up all things in him, things in heaven and things on earth" (Eph. 1:3–10).

Truth 8

We Serve God with Heart *and Mind*

Do not be conformed to this world, but be transformed by the renewing of your minds, so that you may discern what is the will of God.

(Rom. 12:2)

The Life of the Mind
in the Service of Jesus Christ

The life of the mind in the service of Jesus Christ has always been a distinctive hallmark of the Reformed tradition, and it happens to be one of the most exhilarating and deeply satisfying aspects of the Christian life. Yet it also is a challenge. Sometimes, the gospel requires that we call into question beliefs at which we have already arrived, as we open ourselves to brothers and sisters in Christ who have drawn different conclusions. The gospel may indeed lead to a rending of the heart, because it summons us to reexamine some of our strongly held opinions in an effort to open ourselves to the fresh winds of the Holy Spirit.

One thing we must never forget is this: There is always a great distance between God and our finite understanding. We can never presume to have understood everything about God that there is to understand. Never do we know enough to say that. Instead, we are a community of pilgrims who have not yet arrived, but who are constantly on the way "to the city that has foundations, whose architect and builder is God" (Heb. 11:10). Loving God with all the mind, therefore, is a lifelong venture from which one never retires. As Karl Barth has said, one thing is sure: If our understanding of Christian truth "has become small change—pronounced and received as self-evident, already understood, a plausible concept whose meaning is at the disposal of the speaker and hearer as a known factor—then no matter how piously and profoundly the game is played, it is a false game."[1]

When Jesus was asked, "Which commandment is the first of all?" he replied, "The first is, 'Hear, O Israel: the Lord our God, the Lord is one; you shall love the Lord your God with all your heart, and with all your soul, and with all your mind, and with all your strength'" (Mark 12:28–30). Reformed Christians have always taken with utmost seriousness the gospel's call to love and serve God with heart *and mind*, and one of the crying needs of today's church is a renewed commitment to a vigorous use of the intellect in the life of the congregation. It is not readily apparent to those outside the mainline churches that we know what we believe and why we believe it, and many are persuaded that we have so watered down the gospel to make it palatable to every belief and lifestyle that we no longer have any abiding convictions beyond an easy tolerance, thoroughly accommodating to our pluralistic culture. Those inside the church often think that their spirituality is primarily a heart-trip, centered in how they feel about everything under the sun. But the perils of this age remind us that the Christian faith is not only a matter of the heart but also of the head, and God summons us to use the full powers of the mind in thinking through the Christian faith and all of its life-changing implications.

The relativism of American culture is all but unchallenged in the mainline church, and as I have already suggested, it has become sacrosanct never to question the validity or truth of another person's views. There is such a thing as my truth, your truth, her truth, and his truth, but don't you dare suggest that my truth might be wrong! Never mind that, in baptism, we have been yoked to Jesus Christ and, therefore, are accountable to one another in the body of Christ. The real litmus test of a person's credibility these days is measured by her or his openness to every manifestation of diversity quite apart from whether or not it is outside the boundary of Christian truth as revealed in Jesus Christ. One of the results is that we have become enamored of every controversial topic to come down the pike without first stopping to become grounded in God's self-revelation in Jesus Christ, and we have formed so many of our impressive opinions by relying on anything and everything except the Bible and our theological tradition. "This," suggests Thomas Oden, "is like trying to have a baseball game with no rules, no umpire, and no connection with historic baseball."[2] And in such a church as ours, few people these days dare to utter the unthinkable "H" word—heresy. When open-mindedness is presumed to be synonymous with faithfulness, suggesting that someone's views may be heretical is to commit the most grievous of all sins. Oden continues,

But in the "liberated" church circles of old line denominations heresy simply does not exist. After centuries of struggle against recurrent heresies,

Christians have found a quick way of overcoming heresy: they have banished the concept altogether. With absolute relativism holding sway, there is not only no concept of heresy, but no way even to raise the question of where the boundaries of legitimate Christian belief lie.[3]

One day, during a conference of ministers and Christian educators, we were discussing the weals and woes of the church today, and some of those present were outraged at the suggestion that the Christian faith even has boundaries. "The gospel has no boundaries," exclaimed one of the participants with energetic zeal, "the gospel is about removing boundaries." There is a sense, of course, in which that is true, because time-honored boundaries sometimes stifle and kill human relationships by erecting barriers of race and wealth and gender and education and the host of other distinctions that we humans wield with delight. But it does not automatically follow that the gospel itself has no theological boundaries and that the gospel tradition is so open that it can include every belief and lifestyle that anyone chooses to embrace. "Heresy," suggests John Leith, "is not the denial of Christian faith, but the corruption of Christian faith. The heretic is not outside but within the church."[4]

One of our basic jobs as disciples of the risen Christ is to test the prevailing values and mores of our culture against the historic Christian faith. In the words of Christopher Seitz,

> Stripped to the essentials, Christian ministry begins with the capacity to make a robust, intelligent accounting of the faith we hold. Can we state with clarity and conviction what it is that we believe, as this has been handed down to us? What does it mean to say that we worship a crucified and risen Lord? That we believe in a final judgment of the quick and the dead? That we believe the God who created the world is not identical with creation? That we look to Christ's return in glory? Before we move to commend the faith to others in this pluralistic society—however we might do that—can we first state with comprehensiveness and conviction what it is that we ourselves believe, as this has been handed down to us, from Israel to the apostles and from one generation of faith to the next?[5]

What, then, would be an appropriate response in such a time as this? The gospel itself gives us the answer, and it is nothing but the raw and holy cry from the wilderness to prepare the way of the Lord by repentance—turning *from* ourselves *to* God, turning *from* our self-destructive and idolatrous ways *to* the abundant life promised in Jesus Christ, turning *from* our easy answers and feel-good solutions *to* the costly grace of Jesus Christ. It is no accident that the first words that the earliest gospel records from the mouth of Jesus are "The time is fulfilled, and the kingdom of God has come near; repent, and believe in the good news" (Mark 1:15). Repentance and belief in the good news go hand in hand; one does not exist without the other. Furthermore, like the death of the old self and the resurrection to new life, repentance is a repeatable act, an ongoing experience that continually opens us to the transforming power of Jesus Christ. Just as judgment begins in our own house, so also does repentance, and I ask you now to consider the substance of repentance in the context of the life of the mind.

The Renewing of the Mind

In the letter to the Romans, Paul writes, "Do not be conformed to this world, but be transformed by the renewing of your minds, so that you may discern what is the will of God—what is good and acceptable and perfect" (Rom. 12:2). Paul writes, in a similar vein, to the Colossians, "And you who were once estranged and hostile in mind, doing evil deeds, he [Christ] has now reconciled in his fleshly body through death, so as to present you holy and blameless and irreproachable before him" (Col. 1:21–22). Thomas F. Torrance has observed that "the mind of a human being is what the Greeks called . . . the governing principle, for it is the mind that governs or directs our behavior as human beings."[6] In the modern world, we tend to think of the will as the driving force behind human behavior, but

> the Greek Fathers traced everything back to the mind. It is a mistake to think that they were not interested in the will and did not therefore stress the freedom of the will as modern people do, because they laid this emphasis upon the mind as the governing element in human nature. The Greek Fathers realized, however, as perhaps few people do today, that although we may have free will, we are not at all free to escape from our self-will. That is why they put their finger on the twisted state of affairs in the depths of the human mind. It is in the heart of our mental reality which governs and controls all our thinking and culture that we have become estranged from the truth and hostile to God . . . and desperately need to be redeemed and healed.[7]

Thankfully, this is precisely what God has done for us in Jesus Christ. This is the very miracle of grace, the triumph of the cross, the eternal alleluia of Easter. Jesus Christ took the very depths of our depraved minds with him to the cross on Good Friday, and "he descended into the hell of the utmost wickedness and dereliction of the human mind under the judgment of God, in order to lay hold upon the very root of our sin and to redeem us from its stranglehold upon us."[8] Through our redemption in Christ, therefore, the renewal of the mind is now possible. And the miracle of God's infinite love is that our "foul, wicked, depraved humanity, twisted in upon itself . . . [has] been cleansed, changed, redeemed, and sanctified in [the Son of God]."[9] This is the glorious hope of the gospel, the surpassing joy of the children of God.

I hope it is obvious that the life of the mind and the lifelong process of sanctification go hand in hand. Torrance illustrates this point with a wonderful example drawn from the life of a friend. In the years before World War II, Adolf Busch and Rudolf Serkin, two of the world's greatest musicians, were both in Basel, Switzerland, and Torrance's friend, Edgar, who was twenty-seven years old at the time, began taking piano lessons. The great Serkin looked at Edgar's twenty-seven-year-old hands and gave him the sad news that he was too old for him to take on as a student. But, after a time, Serkin sent Edgar to a friend in Salzburg who gave him exercises and, after six months of strenuous work, the muscles in Edgar's hands were completely transformed. As a result, Serkin took him on as a student, and Edgar became a distinguished musician in his own right. He never forgot, however, the agonizing pain that was involved in the restructuring of the muscles in his hands. The saga of Edgar's journey as a pianist illustrates the work of sanctification. It has to do with the Holy Spirit's restructuring of our inner selves, as we "grow up in every way into him who is the head, into Christ" (Eph. 4:15b).

Torrance has often used this account from Edgar's life in explaining to his theological students the renewing of the mind. He tells them, "Something similar may well happen to you in these classes, for as you let the truth of the Gospel have its way with you, you will find the very shape and structure of your mind beginning to change." And that, suggests Torrance, is precisely what repentance is all about: "a radical rethinking of everything before the face of Jesus Christ."[10]

The problem, however, is that we so often cling to the thought patterns of the old self. We accept our greed, for example, as a staple of American life, a reality impossible to escape in the consumerism of today's world. But the truth is, we don't really want to escape it, so we let our comfort with greed rationalize away the call to deny the self, take up our cross, and follow Jesus. The "radical rethinking of everything before the face of Jesus" also should be the very heart and soul of the discussion the church is having over issues that threaten to tear us asunder. No matter which side of which issue we are on, God calls us to rethink the entire matter before the face of Jesus Christ, not first and foremost as a political body maneuvering the system to politick our way to victory, but as *the community of the cross* that looks to Jesus, who is "the way, the truth, and the life" (John 14:6). What do you think might happen if we were to take even the most strife-producing issues and rethink what it means to receive the Bible as God's authoritative Word of truth; rethink what it means to do as Abraham did and "abandon radically all natural roots";[11] rethink what it means to "protest against a world that is fixed on what is safe, predictable, and controllable";[12] rethink what the Bible tells us about love and sex and marriage and money and fidelity in relationships and following Jesus single-mindedly, no matter how much it changes both our convictions and our lifestyles? We tend to embrace the prevailing wisdom of our age too readily. For example, many Christians these days approach such topics as abortion and human sexuality no differently than any other secular person living in our sophisticated world. We frequently reach deeply held convictions about such issues without first bringing the discussion to the One who has both love and power enough to save us from being conformed to this world and to be transformed by the renewing of our minds. How often do congregations take it upon themselves to become centers for the radical rethinking of their relationship with money and status and privilege and family heritage and sex and personal success and marriage and children, by bringing it all under the scrutiny of God's living Word?

The Rich Ruler

In Luke 18:18–30, Jesus is approached by a devoutly religious man. He says, "Good Teacher, what must I do to inherit eternal life?" Jesus answers, "You were reared in the faith; you know the commandments." And the man replies, "You're right, and I have kept them all! In fact, I've lived an exemplary life. When the other kids were getting into trouble, I wasn't. When they created havoc at home, I didn't. I have faithfully kept the law of God since I was a child. I don't lie, I don't steal, I don't cheat, and I never take the Lord's name in vain. I'm proud to say that I know the faith of our ancestors like the back of my hand. But you know what, Jesus? I'm still empty on the inside. Tell me what to do." And Jesus said, "There's one thing causing your spiritual emptiness. You love your possessions too much. In fact, you love your money more than you love God. So I tell you what: Go to your broker and sell all of your stock, then go to the bank and divest yourself of all the CDs in your lock box. Find some people who have been kicked in the teeth by the inequities of life and make their lives better by giving away your money. Once you've done that, and your hands are empty, chances are that you'll be in an entirely different frame of mind. So come back then, and follow me."

As in the life of Abraham, Sarah, and Moses centuries earlier, the rich ruler is summoned to make a radical departure from the past in order to surrender to a new vision of life. What he hadn't bargained for was a divine grace so unbelievably abundant that he would be asked to divest himself of all his golden calves. As difficult as it is for our modern ears to hear the word "exclude," this is exactly what Jesus means. The reign of God *excludes* our golden calves. All options are not open to disciples of Jesus. The Christian faith is not inclusive of all ways of thinking and living. The baggage of the rich ruler's cultural heritage, including his views of God, his neighbor, and even himself, must be surrendered in order to secure the one pearl of great value (Matt. 13:46). Nothing from the past can remain at the center of his life except the desire for faith and obedience. Jesus has in mind the death of the old self and the resurrection to new life, but the rich ruler decides that he is in love with *this* life! So he departs from Jesus and is sorrowful.

Notice that Jesus does not change the meaning of the commandments just so the rich ruler could feel better about himself. No, Jesus says, "Show me an act of surrender; that is the sacrifice which the grace of God inspires. Lay aside everything in life that you treasure more than God, and then come and follow me." This is the heart and soul of what it means that we are saved by grace alone, that "our faith is built upon Thy promise free." Torrance suggests,

> Let us make no mistake about it: divine revelation conflicts sharply with the structure of our natural reason, with the secular patterns of thought that have already become established in our minds through the twist of our ingrained mental alienation from God. We cannot become true theologians without the agonizing experience of profound change in the mental structure of our innermost being. . . . Either you think from out of a mind centered in God through union with the mind of the Lord Jesus, or you think from out of a mind centered in yourself, alienated from God and inwardly hostile to the Truth incarnate in the Lord Jesus, that is, in a way that is finally governed by the unregenerate and unbaptized reason.
>
> The transformation of the human mind and its renewal through assimilation to the mind of Christ is something that has to go on throughout the whole of our life—it is a never-ending discipleship in repentant rethinking as we take up the cross and follow Christ.[13]

The repentant rethinking of everything in the face of Jesus Christ is the gift of divine grace for these troubled times. May this grace of God break forth upon our lives and change us. May it forgive us anew. May it claim us again and again, and call us in each new day. May it burn in our souls until we have given ourselves wholly to God. And may the prayer from John Donne's sonnet be always in our hearts:

> Batter my heart, three person'd God; for, you
> As yet but knock, breathe, shine, and seek to mend;
> That I may rise, and stand, o'erthrow me, and bend
> Your force, to break, blow, burn and make me new.[14]

Postscript

Looking Toward the Future

"Yet Saints Their Watch Are Keeping"

Allow me a brief personal comment as a way of bringing these reflections to a close. I hope it is abundantly clear that, in spite of my frustrations with the life of the church, I love the church and am devoted to our life together. Despite the angst that I often feel over the trials and tribulations of the church, I find that the church frequently gives me hope in the bleakest of moments and bequeaths a sense of divine purpose just when I am tempted to give up. Such, I suppose, is the miracle of God's grace inside this mixed-up, bullheaded, thoroughly human, yet redeemed community of the people of God.

At such moments, I am reminded that God calls me not to be successful, but to be faithful. This, finally, is all God wants from each of us: faithfulness. God wants us to be loyal to Jesus Christ even at the risk of personal vulnerability and sacrifice. God wants us to follow Jesus Christ no matter how hard it is or how futile it seems or how absurd the whole thing appears to become. *For the gift of following the risen Christ is the supreme joy of divine grace.*

In this mass of humanity gathered at the foot of the cross, I am reminded that we are brothers and sisters in Christ, and as Dietrich Bonhoeffer says in *Life Together*, we come to each other *through the mediator, Jesus Christ.*[1] By the grace of God, the cross of Jesus stands between us to love us and forgive us and reform us and keep on loving us and forgiving us and reforming us. His cross is our only hope, our only joy, our only tomorrow. I am reminded of the immense comfort I experience each time we sing that great hymn of the church, "The Church's One Foundation." The third stanza speaks an eloquent and powerful word to the mixed-up times in which we live:

> Though with a scornful wonder this world sees her oppressed,
> By schisms rent asunder, by heresies distressed,

Yet saints their watch are keeping; their cry goes up "How long?"
And soon the night of weeping shall be the morn of song.[2]

Indeed, saints their watch *are* keeping. For "we are surrounded by so great a cloud of witnesses" (Heb. 12:1) who sing the eternal victory of Jesus Christ in ceaseless doxology.

> Jesus is Lord!
> He has been Lord from the beginning.
> He will be Lord at the end.
> Even now he is Lord.[3]

Notes

INTRODUCTION: FORGOTTEN TRUTH

1. Karl Barth, *A Karl Barth Reader*, ed. Rolf Joachim Erler and Reiner Marquard, trans. Geoffrey W. Bromiley (Grand Rapids: Wm. B. Eerdmans Pub. Co., 1986), 39.
2. James D. Smart, *The Strange Silence of the Bible in the Church* (Philadelphia: Westminster Press, 1970).
3. When speaking of the Reformed tradition, I refer to the theological tradition with roots in the teachings of John Calvin during the Protestant Reformation of the sixteenth century. The Protestant Reformation was sparked by Martin Luther in 1517 as an endeavor to reform the church by recovering the beliefs and practices of the ancient catholic church based on the Bible.
4. The Heidelberg Catechism, *Book of Confessions* (Louisville, Ky.: Geneva Press, 1996), 4.001. The Constitution of the Presbyterian Church (U.S.A.) is made up of two documents: the *Book of Confessions* (Part I), and the *Book of Order* (Part II). The *Book of Confessions* is the doctrinal part of the Constitution; the *Book of Order* deals with church government. The role of the *Book of Confessions* in the life of the church is explained in greater detail in "Truth 6, God Is Revealed in the Bible."
5. John Calvin, *Institutes of the Christian Religion*, ed. John T. McNeill, trans. Ford Lewis Battles (Philadelphia: Westminster Press, 1960), III.7.1.
6. P. T. Forsyth, *Positive Preaching and the Modern Mind* (London: Independent Press LTD, 1907), 23.
7. Elizabeth Achtemeier, "Renewed Appreciation for an Unchanging Story," *The Christian Century*, June 13–20, 1990, 599.
8. "Those Mainline Blues," reported by Jordan Bonfante, Barbara Dolan, and Michael P. Harris, *Time*, May 22, 1989, 94.
9. Herbert O'Driscoll, "The View from the Hill of Mars," Hastings Memorial Lecture MCMXCVIII (Washington, D.C.: College of Preachers, Washington National Cathedral, 1998), 15.
10. Ibid.
11. John Leith, *Introduction to the Reformed Tradition*, rev. ed. (Atlanta: John Knox Press, 1981), 31. Leith is quoting Jaroslav Pelikan.
12. Henry Williams Baker, "The King of Love My Shepherd Is," *The Presbyterian Hymnal: Hymns, Psalms, and Spiritual Songs* (Louisville, Ky.: Westminster/John Knox Press, 1990), 171.

LAYING THE FOUNDATION: GETTING THE BIBLE WHOLE

1. Katherine Hankey, "I Love to Tell the Story," *The Hymnbook* (Richmond, Philadelphia, and New York: Presbyterian Church in the U.S., United Presbyterian Church in the U.S.A., and Reformed Church in America, 1955), 383.
2. James Weldon Johnson, "Creation," *God's Trombones* (New York: Penguin Books, 1927), 20.
3. Gerhard von Rad, *Genesis* (Philadelphia: Westminster Press, 1961), 58.
4. Terrence E. Fretheim, *Genesis*, The New Interpreter's Bible, Vol. 1 (Nashville: Abingdon Press, 1994), 345.
5. Cf. Shirley Guthrie, *Christian Doctrine*, rev. ed. (Louisville, Ky.: Westminster John Knox Press, 1994), 150, and Walter Brueggemann, *Genesis* (Atlanta: John Knox Press, 1982), 32.
6. Arthur Campbell Ainger, "God Is Working His Purpose Out," *The Hymnbook*, 500.
7. African-American spiritual, "Were You There?" *The Presbyterian Hymnal: Hymns, Psalms, and Spiritual Songs* (Louisville, Ky.: Westminster/John Knox Press, 1990), 102.
8. John H. Leith, *Introduction to the Reformed Tradition*, rev. ed. (Atlanta: John Knox Press, 1981), 26–27.

TRUTH 1: GOD IS IN CHARGE

1. Shirley C. Guthrie, "Human Suffering, Human Liberation, and the Sovereignty of God," *Theology Today* 53, no. 1 (April 1996): 23.
2. The Westminster Confession of Faith, *Book of Confessions* (Louisville, Ky.: Geneva Press, 1996), 6.014.
3. John Calvin, *Institutes of the Christian Religion*, ed. John T. McNeill, trans. Ford Lewis Battles (Philadelphia: Westminster Press, 1960), I.16.3.
4. Ibid., I.16.3.
5. Ibid., I.16.8.
6. Guthrie, "Human Suffering," 23.
7. Ibid., 25.
8. John Ellerton, "The Day Thou Gavest, Lord, Is Ended," *The Presbyterian Hymnal: Hymns, Psalms, and Spiritual Songs* (Louisville, Ky.: Westminster/John Knox Press, 1990), 546.
9. Robert Farrar Capon, *The Parables of the Kingdom* (Grand Rapids: Zondervan Publishing House, 1985), 20.
10. Ibid., 22.
11. Ibid., 23.
12. Frederick Buechner, "The Power of God and the Power of Man," *The Magnificent Defeat* (New York: Seabury Press, 1966), 34.
13. Karl Barth, *The Humanity of God*, trans. John Newton Thomas and Thomas Wieser (Richmond, Va.: John Knox Press, 1960), 48–49.
14. Charles Wesley, "Hark! The Herald Angels Sing," *The Presbyterian Hymnal*, 31.
15. John Francis Wade, "O Come, All Ye Faithful," *The Presbyterian Hymnal*, 41.
16. Karl Barth, *The Humanity of God*, 48–49.
17. Henry Francis Lyte, "Praise, My Soul, the King of Heaven," *The Presbyterian Hymnal*, 478.

18. William Sloane Coffin Jr., "Alex's Death," *A Chorus of Witnesses*, ed. Thomas G. Long and Cornelius Plantinga Jr. (Grand Rapids: Wm. B. Eerdmans Pub. Co., 1994), 263–264.

19. John Leith, *Introduction to the Reformed Tradition*, rev. ed. (Atlanta: John Knox Press, 1981), 70.

20. Ibid., 71.

21. The Westminster Shorter Catechism, *Book of Confessions*, 7.001.

22. Leith, *Introduction to the Reformed Tradition*, 99.

23. Karl Barth, *The Faith of the Church: A Commentary on the Apostles' Creed According to Calvin's Catechism* (New York: Meridian Books, 1958), 137.

24. John Calvin, *Letters of John Calvin*, vol. 1, ed. Jules Bonner (New York: B. Franklin, 1973), 280–281.

25. William Barclay, *A Book of Everyday Prayers* (New York: Harper & Brothers, 1959), 113–114.

26. David Buttrick, quoted in "God Is Coming," *Pulpit Resource*, Logos Productions, Inc., November 27, 1994.

TRUTH 2: GOD CALLS US TO BE A HOLY PEOPLE

1. The Westminster Confession of Faith, *Book of Confessions* (Louisville, Ky.: Geneva Press, 1996), 6.016.

2. Cf. John Calvin, *Institutes of the Christian Religion*, ed. John T. McNeill, trans. Ford Lewis Battles (Philadelphia: Westminster Press, 1960), III.21.

3. John H. Leith, *An Introduction to the Reformed Tradition*, rev. ed. (Atlanta: John Knox Press, 1981), 104–105.

4. Karl Barth, *The Humanity of God*, trans. John Newton Thomas and Thomas Wieser (Richmond, Va.: John Knox Press, 1960), 50.

5. John Newton, "Amazing Grace," *The Presbyterian Hymnal: Hymns, Psalms, and Spiritual Songs* (Louisville, Ky.: Westminster/John Knox Press, 1990), 280.

6. William Ernest Henley, "Invictus," *The New Oxford Book of English Verse*, ed. Helen Gardner (New York and Oxford: Oxford University Press, 1972), 792.

7. Leith, *An Introduction to the Reformed Tradition*, 105.

8. John H. Leith, *Basic Christian Doctrine* (Louisville, Ky.: Westminster/John Knox Press, 1993), 226.

9. Read Genesis 11:27–25:11 for the narrative of Abraham and Sarah, as well as the reference to them in Hebrews 11:8–11.

10. Walter Brueggemann, *Genesis* (Atlanta: John Knox Press, 1982), 105.

11. Gerhard von Rad, *Genesis*, trans. John H. Marks (Philadelphia: Westminster Press, 1961), 154.

12. Ibid., 157.

13. Ibid., 154.

14. Brueggemann, *Genesis*, 111.

15. Ibid., 106.

16. Ibid., 111.

17. Shirley C. Guthrie, "Human Suffering, Human Liberation, and the Sovereignty of God," *Theology Today* 53, no. 1 (April 1996): 28.

18. Brueggemann, *Genesis*, 105.

19. Read Exodus 3:1–4:17 for the call of Moses, as well as the reference to him in Hebrews 11:27.

20. The Second Helvetic Confession, *Book of Confessions*, 5.060.

21. Calvin, *Institutes,* III.22.1.

22. Lesslie Newbigin, *A Word in Season* (Grand Rapids: Wm. B. Eerdmans Pub. Co., and Edinburgh: Saint Andrew Press, 1994), 79.

23. Karl Barth, *Church Dogmatics* II/2, trans. G. W. Bromiley et al., ed. G. W. Bromiley and T. F. Torrance (Edinburgh: T.&T. Clark, 1957), 415, 419.

24. The Second Helvetic Confession, *Book of Confessions*, 5.055.

TRUTH 3: JESUS CHRIST REVEALS GOD'S LOVE

1. John R. Claypool, "Mutiny, Easter and the Table," *Lectionary Homiletics* 7, no. 11 (October 1996): 9.

2. Saint Augustine, *The Confessions of Saint Augustine*, 8.7, as quoted by Walter J. Burghardt, "Advent: Remember, Repent, Rehearse," *The Living Pulpit* 6, no. 4 (October–December 1997): 4–5.

3. Johann Heermann, "An Holy Jesus, How Hast Thou Offended," *The Hymnbook* (Richmond, Philadelphia, and New York: Presbyterian Church in the U.S., the United Presbyterian Church in the U.S.A., and Reformed Church in America, 1955), 191.

4. T. S. Eliot, *The Cocktail Party* (New York: Harcourt, Brace & World, 1950), 111.

5. John Calvin, *Institutes of the Christian Religion*, ed. John T. McNeill, trans. Ford Lewis Battles (Philadelphia: Westminster Press, 1960), II.1.2.

6. Robert L. Russell, "Where Are My Strengths," *Preaching* 12, no. 1 (July–August, 1996): 13.

7. "There Is a Balm in Gilead," African-American spiritual, *The Presbyterian Hymnal: Hymns, Psalms, and Spiritual Songs* (Louisville, Ky.: Westminster/John Knox Press, 1990), 394.

8. Cf. Matthew 9:12 and Mark 2:17 where a variation of this statement also occurs.

9. Fanny J. Crosby, "I Am Thine, O Lord," *The Presbyterian Hymnal* (Richmond, Va.: Presbyterian Committee of Publication, 1927), 217.

10. Gary A. Anderson, "Necessarium Adae Peccatum: The Problem of Original Sin," in *Sin, Death, and the Devil*, ed. Carl E. Braaten and Robert W. Jenson (Grand Rapids: Wm. B. Eerdmans Pub. Co., 2000), 39. Anderson is here reflecting on Karl Barth's treatment of the doctrine of original sin, *Church Dogmatics* IV.

11. Elizabeth Cecilia Douglas Clephane, "Beneath the Cross of Jesus," *The Presbyterian Hymnal*, 92.

12. *The Book of Common Worship* (Philadelphia: Office of the General Assembly of the Presbyterian Church in the U.S.A., 1946), 12.

13. Read Genesis 3 for the introduction of sin into the biblical story.

14. Edward T. Oakes, "Original Sin: A Disputation," *First Things* 87 (November 1998): 16.

15. Shirley Guthrie, *Christian Doctrine,* rev. ed. (Louisville, Ky.: Westminster John Knox Press, 1994), 221.

16. Read 2 Samuel 11:1–12:15a for the story of David and Bathsheba as well as David's encounter with the prophet Nathan.

17. Cf. Psalm 51. Tradition holds that this is the prayer David prayed after his encounter with the prophet Nathan.

18. Westminster Shorter Catechism, *The Book of Confessions* (Louisville, Ky.: Geneva Press, 1996), 7.014.

19. Shirley Guthrie, *Christian Doctrine*, 215.

20. Emil Brunner, *Man in Revolt: A Christian Anthropology*, trans. Olive Wyon (London: Lutterworth Press, 1939), 129.

21. Ibid., 130.

22. Ibid., 132.

23. Ibid.

24. Brett Younger, "In Praise of Doubt," Theological Web Publishing, LLC, http://www.ser monmall.com/TheMall/99/apr99/041199m.html.

25. Brunner, *Man in Revolt,* 136–137.

26. Ibid., 136.

27. *The Book of Common Worship,* 12.

28. Let me suggest that, if you have not already done so, you stop now and read the story of the suffering, death, and resurrection of Jesus in one or more of the four Gospels: Matthew 26:1–28:10; Mark 14:12–16:8; Luke 22:1–24:12; John 18:1–20:18.

29. Scholars identify four Servant Songs in Isaiah: 42:1–4; 49:1–6; 50:4–11; 52:13–53:12.

30. This explanation of the four images of the atoneement comes from Guthrie, *Christian Doctrine*, 252–256.

31. Martin Luther, "A Mighty Fortress Is Our God," *The Presbyterian Hymnal*, 260.

32. Quoted by S. Mark Heim, "Christ Crucified," *The Christian Century* 118, no. 8 (March 7, 2001): 12. This statement is attributed to one of the speakers at a Re-imagining Conference, held in Minneapolis, MN, November 4–7, 1993.

33. Jürgen Moltmann, *The Crucified God* (New York: Harper & Row, 1974), 204.

34. The phrase "death is dead" is from Eugene O'Neill, *Lazarus Laughed,* published in *Nine Plays by Eugene O'Neill* (New York: The Modern Library, 1941), 427.

35. Karl Barth, *Dogmatics in Outline* (New York: Harper & Brothers, 1959), 123.

36. David H. C. Read, "Unfinished Easter," *Unfinished Easter: Sermons on the Ministry* (San Francisco: Harper & Row, 1978), 96–102.

TRUTH 4: GOD'S LOVE IS NOT FOR SALE

1. John Calvin, "I Greet Thee, Who My Sure Redeemer Art," *The Presbyterian Hymnal: Hymns, Psalms, and Spiritual Songs* (Louisville, Ky.: Westminster/John Knox Press, 1990), 457.

2. Williston Walker, *A History of the Christian Church*, 3d ed. (New York: Charles Scribner's Sons, 1970), 302–303.

3. Martin Luther, *Luther's Works, Sermons I*, vol. 51, ed. Helmut T. Lehmann (Muhlenberg Press, 1959), 14. Cf. Douglas John Hall, *Lighten Our Darkness* (Philadelphia: Westminster Press, 1976), 117, for his treatment of this quote.

4. Quoted by Hall, *Lighten Our Darkness*, 117. The quote is from the writing of Martin Luther, dated Tuesday, February 16, 1546, two days before his death.

5. Hall, *Lighten Our Darkness*, 117.

6. Karl Barth, *Church Dogmatics* IV/1, trans. G. W. Bromiley, ed. G. W. Bromiley and T. F. Torrance (Edinburgh: T.&T. Clark, 1956), 615–617.

7. I am indebted in this section to George W. Stroup and to comments he made in a lecture at Adult Christian Training in Grace Presbytery, September 1991, the notes of which are in my files.

8. Cf. Robert Farrar Capon, *The Parables of Judgment* (Grand Rapids: Wm. B. Eerdmans Pub. Co., 1989), 53–54, who suggests that the Greek word translated "Friend" in this passage and elsewhere in the New Testament is a distinctly unfriendly word, meaning something like "Buster."

9. John Calvin, *Institutes of the Christian Religion*, ed. John T. McNeill, trans. Ford Lewis Battles (Philadelphia: Westminster Press, 1960), III.2.7.

10. Capon, *Parables of Judgment*, 55.

11. Walker, *A History of the Christian Church*, 168.

12. Shirley Guthrie, *Christian Doctrine*, rev. ed. (Louisville, Ky.: Westminster John Knox Press, 1994), 126.

13. *The Oxford Dictionary of the Christian Church*, 3d ed., ed. F. L. Cross and E. A. Livingstone (Oxford: Oxford University Press, 1997), 1481.

14. Guthrie, *Christian Doctrine*, 127–128.

15. Barth, *Church Dogmatics*, IV/1, 631–633.

16. William Temple, *Nature, Man and God* (London: Macmillan & Co., 1934), 401.

17. Isaac Watts, "When I Survey the Wondrous Cross," *The Presbyterian Hymnal*, 101.

18. Calvin, *Institutes*, III.11.7.

19. Barth, *Church Dogmatics*, IV/1, 631.

TRUTH 5: GOD GIVES NEW LIFE

1. Anne Tyler, *Saint Maybe* (New York: Ivy Books, 1991), 47–49, 125–138, 231.

2. John Calvin, *Institutes of the Christian Religion*, ed. John T. McNeill, trans. Ford Lewis Battles (Philadelphia: Westminster Press, 1960), III.7.8.

3. William H. Willimon, *Peculiar Speech* (Grand Rapids: Wm. B. Eerdmans Pub. Co., 1992), 119.

4. Philip Yancey, *I Was Just Wondering* (Grand Rapids: Wm. B. Eerdmans Pub. Co., 1989), 211.

5. *The Book of Common Worship* (Philadelphia: Office of the General Assembly of the Presbyterian Church in the U.S.A., 1946), 178.

6. Shirley Guthrie, *Christian Doctrine*, rev. ed. (Louisville, Ky.: Westminster John Knox Press, 1994), 331.

7. Dietrich Bonhoeffer, *The Cost of Discipleship* (New York: Macmillan Co., 1937), 69.

8. W. H. Auden, "For the Time Being," *Collected Poems* (New York: Random House, 1969), 303.

9. Bonhoeffer, *The Cost of Discipleship*, 45, 47.

10. C. S. Lewis, *Mere Christianity* (New York: Macmillan Co., Inc., 1943), 167.

11. Westminster Shorter Catechism, *Book of Confessions* (Louisville, Ky.: Geneva Press, 1996), 7.001.

12. John H. Leith, *An Introduction to the Reformed Tradition*, 72. Leith's reference is from Nicolas Berdyaev, *The Destiny of Man* (New York: Charles Scribner's Sons, 1937), 146.

13. Cornelius Plantinga Jr., *Not the Way It's Supposed to Be: A Breviary of Sin* (Grand Rapids: Wm. B. Eerdmans Pub. Co., 1995), 83.

14. Calvin, *Institutes*, III.7.2.

15. Ibid., III.7.4.

16. Bonhoeffer, *The Cost of Discipleship*, 63.

17. Ibid., 99.

18. Alan Paton, *Ah, But Your Land Is Beautiful* (New York: Charles Scribner's Sons, 1981), 66.

19. Karl Barth, *Church Dogmatics*, IV/1 (trans. G. W. Bromiley, ed. G. W. Bromiley and T. F. Torrance (Edinburgh: T.&T. Clark, 1956), 627.

20. *Time* magazine as quoted by Walter J. Burghardt, "A Brother Whom I Have Pardoned," *The Living Pulpit* 3, no. 2 (April–June 1994): 10.

21. Isaac Watts, "So Let Our Lips and Lives Express," *The Hymnbook* (Richmond, Philadelphia, and New York: Presbyterian Church in the U.S., Presbyterian Church in the U.S.A., and Reformed Church in America, 1955), 289.

22. Martin Luther, "Treatise on Christian Liberty," *Works of Martin Luther*, vol. 2 (Muhlenberg), 331, as quoted in Robert McAfee Brown, *The Spirit of Protestantism* (London, Oxford, and New York: Oxford University Press, 1961), 65.

23. Desmond M. Tutu, "The Best for Our Family," *The Living Pulpit* 2, no. 1 (January–March 1993): 25.

24. Martin Luther, *Weimarer Ausgabe,* vol. 7, 35, 25ff, cited in Nygren, *Agape and Eros*, Part II, Vol. II, 509, as quoted in Robert McAfee Brown, *The Spirit of Protestantism* (London, Oxford, and New York: Oxford University Press, 1961), 65–66.

TRUTH 6: GOD IS REVEALED IN THE BIBLE

1. *Book of Order* (Louisville, Ky.: Office of the General Assembly of the Presbyterian Church [U.S.A.], 2000), G-14.0802.

2. The Confession of 1967, *Book of Confessions* (Louisville, Ky.: Geneva Press, 1996), 9.27.

3. The Larger Catechism, *Book of Confessions*, 7.113, 7.115.

4. Robert Bellah, et al., *Habits of the Heart—Individualism and Commitment in American Life* (Berkeley: University of California Press, 1985), 221.

5. Eugene H. Peterson, "Eat This Book, The Holy Community at Table with the Holy Scripture," *Theology Today* 56, no. 1 (April 1999): 5.

6. Ibid., 5.

7. Cf. chapters 1 and 2 of the Second Helvetic Confession, and chapter 1 of the Westminster Confession of Faith for additional affirmations concerning the interpretation of scripture.

8. Karl Barth, *Dogmatics in Outline* (New York: Harper & Brothers, 1959), 13.

9. John Calvin, *Institutes of the Christian Religion*, ed. John T. McNeill, trans. Ford Lewis Battles (Philadelphia: Westminster Press, 1960), I.1.2.

10. Calvin, *Institutes,* I.7.4 and I.9.3. Cf. Karl Barth, *Church Dogmatics*, I/2, trans. G. W. Bromiley, ed. G. W. Bromiley and T. F. Torrance (Edinburgh: T.&T. Clark, 1956), 457.

11. The Westminster Confession of Faith, *Book of Confessions*, 6.005–6.006.

12. The Confession of 1967, *Book of Confessions*, 9.27–9.30.

13. *The Service for the Lord's Day*, Supplemental Liturgical Resource 1 (Philadelphia: Westminster Press, 1984), 59.

14. The Confession of 1967, *Book of Confessions*, 9.29.

15. Barth, *Dogmatics in Outline*, 13.

16. The Theological Declaration of Barmen, *Book of Confessions*, 8.11.

17. The Confession of 1967, *Book of Confessions*, 9.29.

18. Cf. the discussion of the Acts passage in Peter Gomes, *The Good Book* (New York: William Morrow & Co., 1996), 32–33.

19. Barth, *Dogmatics in Outline*, 13.
20. From a lecture on Reformed theology that George W. Stroup gave in Grace Presbytery at Adult Christian Training, September 1991.
21. Barth, *Church Dogmatics*, I/2, 606–607.
22. Ibid., 538.
23. Ibid., 589–590.
24. Ibid., 588.
25. The Westminster Confession of Faith, *Book of Confessions*, 6.009.
26. Calvin, *Institutes,* I.6.1.
27. Peterson, "Eat This Book," 6.
28. Carlos E. Wilton, "A Witness for the Defense," Theological Web Publishing, LLC, http://www.sermonmall.com/TheMall/00/may00/050700a.html.

TRUTH 7: WE ARE THE CHURCH TOGETHER

1. *The Oxford Dictionary of the Christian Church*, ed. F. L. Cross, 3d. ed., ed. E. A. Livingstone (Oxford: Oxford University Press, 1997), 1253.
2. Cf. Acts 9:1–22 for the account of Saul's Damascus Road experience.
3. Browne Barr, *High-Flying Geese: Unexpected Reflections on the Church & Its Ministry* (Minneapolis: Seabury Press, 1983), 8.
4. "The Domestic Goose—a moral tale," *The Journals of Søren Kierkegaard*, ed. and trans. Alexander Dru (London: Oxford University Press, 1938), 541, quoted by Brown Barr, *High-Flying Geese*, 8–9.
5. T. S. Eliot, "The Love Song of J. Alfred Prufrock," *The Heath Anthology of American Literature*, vol. 2, 1st ed., ed. Paul Lauter (Lexington, Mass.: D. C. Heath & Co., 1990), 1302.
6. *Book of Order*, (Louisville, Ky.: Office of the General Assembly of the Presbyterian Church [U.S.A.], 2000), G-3.0200.
7. Cf. *Book of Order*, G-3.0200.
8. George Gallup Jr. and D. Michael Lindsay, *Surveying the Religious Landscape* (Harrisburg, Pa.: Morehouse Publishing Co., 1999), 4.
9. David F. Wells, *No Place for Truth or Whatever Happened to Evangelical Theology?* (Grand Rapids: Wm. B. Eerdmans Pub. Co., 1993), 183.
10. *The Interpreter's Dictionary of the Bible*, vol. 1 (Nashville: Abingdon Press, 1962), 715.
11. Ibid., 607.
12. John Calvin, *Institutes of the Christian Religion*, ed. John T. McNeill, trans. Ford Lewis Battles (Philadelphia: Westminster Press, 1960), IV.1.1, IV.1.4.
13. Shirley Guthrie, *Christian Doctrine*, rev. ed. (Louisville, Ky.: Westminster John Knox Press, 1994), 355–356.
14. Kenneth E. Bailey, *Through Peasant Eyes* (Grand Rapids: Wm. B. Eerdmans Pub. Co., 1976), 26.
15. John Fawcett, "Blest Be the Tie That Binds," *The Presbyterian Hymnal: Hymns, Psalms, and Spiritual Songs* (Louisville, Ky.: Westminster/John Knox Press, 1990), 438.
16. John Killinger, "God Doesn't Have Any Orphans!" Theological Web Publishers, LLC, http://www.sermonmall.com/TheMall/00/may00/052100q.html.
17. Albert Curry Winn, *A Sense of Mission: Guidance from the Gospel of John* (Philadelphia: Westminster Press, 1981), 55.

18. Calvin, *Institutes,* IV.1.9.
19. Ibid., IV.14.5.
20. Cf. The Westminster Confession of Faith, *Book of Confessions*, 6.140–6.145.
21. Samuel John Stone, "The Church's One Foundation," *The Presbyterian Hymnal* 442.

TRUTH 8: WE SERVE GOD WITH HEART *AND MIND*

1. Karl Barth, *A Karl Barth Reader*, ed. Rolf Joachim Erler and Reiner Marquard, trans. Geoffrey W. Bromiley (Grand Rapids: Wm. B. Eerdmans Pub. Co., 1986), 6.
2. Thomas Oden, "Can We Talk about Hesesy?" *The Christian Century*, April 12, 1995, 390.
3. Ibid.
4. John H. Leith, *Crisis in the Church* (Louisville, Ky.: Westminster John Knox Press, 1997), 36.
5. Christopher Seitz, "Pluralism and the Lost Art of Apology," *First Things* (June–July 1994): 16.
6. Thomas F. Torrance, "The Reconciliation of Mind: A Theological Meditation upon the Teaching of St. Paul," in *Theology in the Service of the Church: Essays in Honor of Thomas W. Gillespie*, ed. Wallace M. Alston Jr. (Grand Rapids: Wm. B. Eerdmans Pub. Co., 2000), 197.
7. Ibid., 197–198.
8. Ibid., 198–199.
9. Ibid., 200.
10. Ibid., 200–201.
11. Gerhard von Rad, *Genesis*, trans. John H. Marks (Philadelphia: Westminster Press, 1961), 154.
12. Walter Brueggemann, *Genesis* (Atlanta: John Knox Press, 1982), 111.
13. Torrance, "The Reconciliation of Mind," 201, 203.
14. John Donne, "Holy Sonnet 171," *The Complete Poetry of John Donne*, ed. John T. Shawcross (Garden City, N.Y.: Anchor Books, Doubleday & Co., 1967), 344.

POSTSCRIPT: LOOKING TOWARD THE FUTURE

1. Dietrich Bonhoeffer, *Life Together* (New York and Evanston, Ill.: Harper & Row, 1954), 21.
2. Samuel John Stone, "The Church's One Foundation," *The Presbyterian Hymnal: Hymns, Songs, and Spiritual Songs* (Louisville, Ky.: Westminster/John Knox Press, 1990), 442.
3. "A Declaration of Faith" (Presbyterian Church in the United States, 1977), 10.5.